True Stories of Aviation Disasters & Mysteries

Shah Rukh

Published by Shah Rukh, 2024.

TRUE STORIES OF AVIATION DISASTERS & MYSTERIES

First edition. June 1, 2024.

Written by Shah Rukh.

Table of Contents

Prologue

Aviation, since its inception, has been a symbol of human ingenuity and progress. The sky, once a domain only for the birds, has become a realm of technological marvels, connecting the world in ways unimaginable a century ago. The hum of jet engines, the graceful arc of a plane across the sky, and the bustling activity of airports are now familiar sights and sounds, representing the promise of exploration, commerce, and human connection.

However, with the great strides in aviation have come profound tragedies and enduring mysteries. Each chapter of aviation history is punctuated with incidents that have left indelible marks on our collective memory. These stories, often shrouded in a blend of sorrow, intrigue, and resilience, are reminders of the inherent risks that accompany the quest to conquer the skies.

This book, "True Stories of Aviation Disasters & Mysteries," is a journey through the annals of aviation history, exploring fifty of the most significant and enigmatic cases. From the perplexing disappearance of Amelia Earhart to the unresolved enigma of Malaysia Airlines Flight MH370, each chapter delves into a story that has captured the world's attention. These accounts not only chronicle the events themselves but also honor the memories of those who were lost and examine the lasting impact on aviation safety and regulation.

In these pages, you will find tales of human error and mechanical failure, of natural disasters and acts of terrorism. You will encounter mysteries that defy explanation and heroism in the face of unimaginable adversity. The stories are diverse, yet each one shares a common thread: the unyielding quest for answers and the relentless pursuit of improvement in aviation safety.

As you read through these chapters, you will gain insights into the complexities of air travel, the challenges faced by those who investigate these tragedies, and the technological advancements driven by the need to prevent future disasters. More importantly, you will bear witness to the human stories behind the headlines—the passengers, crew members, investigators, and families who have been forever changed by these events.

"True Stories of Aviation Disasters & Mysteries" is not just a chronicle of past events; it is a tribute to the resilience of the human spirit and a testament to our enduring quest for knowledge and safety in the skies. As we embark on this journey together, let us remember and honor those who have been lost and strive to learn from each tragedy, ensuring that the sky remains a place of wonder and connection for generations to come.

Chapter 1: Amelia Earhart's Disappearance

Amelia Earhart's disappearance remains one of the most enduring mysteries in the history of aviation. Born on July 24, 1897, Earhart became a pioneering aviator and a symbol of women's progress in the field. Her legacy includes numerous flying records, including being the first woman to fly solo across the Atlantic Ocean. However, it is her fateful attempt to circumnavigate the globe in 1937 that has cemented her place in history as an enigmatic figure whose disappearance has fascinated generations.

Earhart embarked on her round-the-world flight on June 1, 1937, from Oakland, California, with her navigator, Fred Noonan. They aimed to fly about 29,000 miles and make multiple stops across several continents. The aircraft chosen for this ambitious journey was a Lockheed Model 10-E Electra, a state-of-the-art twin-engine monoplane capable of long-distance flight. The flight plan took them across South America, Africa, the Indian subcontinent, and Southeast Asia, navigating through some of the most challenging and isolated parts of the world.

By late June, Earhart and Noonan had successfully covered approximately 22,000 miles, with only 7,000 miles remaining. On July 2, 1937, they took off from Lae, New Guinea, heading for Howland Island, a tiny uninhabited coral atoll in the central Pacific Ocean. This leg of the journey, around 2,556 miles, was fraught with danger due to the vast expanse of open water and the limited navigational aids available at the time. Howland Island, their intended destination, was no more than a speck in the ocean, increasing the difficulty of the navigation.

To assist with their navigation and ensure a successful landing, the U.S. Coast Guard cutter Itasca was stationed off Howland Island.

The Itasca was to provide radio communication and direction-finding services to guide Earhart and Noonan. However, numerous problems arose during this critical phase. Communication between Earhart and the Itasca was erratic and plagued by misunderstandings. Earhart's radio transmissions were received by the Itasca, but the signals were weak and often indecipherable. Conversely, it appeared that Earhart and Noonan were unable to hear the transmissions from the Itasca clearly, complicating their navigation efforts.

The last confirmed radio transmission from Earhart was received at 8:43 a.m. on July 2, 1937. Earhart reported, "We are on the line 157 337. We will repeat this message. We will repeat this on 6210 kilocycles. Wait." This cryptic message suggested that they were flying along a line of position running northwest to southeast, which intersected Howland Island. Despite repeated attempts to re-establish contact, no further messages were received. Subsequent efforts by the Itasca to communicate with Earhart were met with silence.

The disappearance of Earhart and Noonan triggered an extensive search and rescue operation, one of the largest and most costly in history at the time. The U.S. Navy and Coast Guard scoured the surrounding areas of the Pacific Ocean, deploying ships, aircraft, and submarines in a desperate bid to locate the missing aviators. Despite these exhaustive efforts, no trace of Earhart, Noonan, or their aircraft was ever found. On July 19, 1937, the search was officially called off, and Earhart and Noonan were declared lost at sea.

Over the decades, numerous theories and speculations have emerged about what might have happened to Earhart and Noonan. One of the most widely accepted theories is that their plane ran out of fuel, forcing them to ditch into the ocean, where they perished. The vast expanse of the Pacific, coupled with the limited technology of the era, made it nearly impossible to locate their remains or the wreckage of the plane.

Another theory posits that Earhart and Noonan might have crash-landed on a remote island in the Pacific, such as Gardner Island (now Nikumaroro) in the Phoenix Islands. This theory gained some support from the discovery of artifacts on the island, including a piece of plexiglass that might have come from an aircraft window and an aluminum panel similar to those used on Earhart's Electra. In addition, bones found on the island in 1940, initially dismissed as those of a male, have been re-examined and are now considered to possibly belong to Earhart. However, definitive proof remains elusive.

Conspiracy theories also abound, with some suggesting that Earhart was captured by Japanese forces, either accidentally or as part of a covert mission, and taken to the Marshall Islands or Saipan. According to this theory, Earhart and Noonan were either executed or died in captivity. While intriguing, these theories lack substantial evidence and are often dismissed by historians and experts.

Efforts to solve the mystery of Earhart's disappearance continue to this day. Modern expeditions, equipped with advanced technology such as underwater drones and high-resolution sonar, have explored potential crash sites in the Pacific Ocean and on remote islands. Organizations like The International Group for Historic Aircraft Recovery (TIGHAR) have dedicated years to investigating the Nikumaroro hypothesis, conducting multiple expeditions and research studies.

Amelia Earhart's legacy endures not only because of her groundbreaking achievements in aviation but also because of the enduring mystery surrounding her final flight. Her disappearance remains a symbol of the challenges and dangers faced by early aviators, as well as the human spirit's unyielding quest for exploration and discovery. Despite the passage of time and numerous investigations, the fate of Amelia Earhart and Fred Noonan remains one of the great unsolved mysteries of the 20th century, continuing to captivate and inspire new generations of aviators, historians, and adventurers.

Chapter 2: Malaysia Airlines Flight MH370

Malaysia Airlines Flight MH370, a Boeing 777-200ER, disappeared on March 8, 2014, while flying from Kuala Lumpur International Airport in Malaysia to Beijing Capital International Airport in China. The aircraft, carrying 227 passengers and 12 crew members, vanished from radar screens less than an hour after takeoff, marking one of the most perplexing and tragic mysteries in aviation history.

The flight departed Kuala Lumpur at 12:41 a.m. local time. Communication between the cockpit and air traffic control was normal until the last transmission, which came at 1:19 a.m., when Captain Zaharie Ahmad Shah said, "Good night Malaysian three seven zero." At 1:21 a.m., the aircraft's transponder, which relays information about the plane's location and altitude, was turned off as it crossed into Vietnamese airspace over the South China Sea. The plane then deviated from its planned route, turning westward back across the Malay Peninsula and heading into the Andaman Sea. Military radar tracked this unusual flight path until the aircraft disappeared from radar at 2:22 a.m., over the Andaman Sea, northwest of Penang Island.

The immediate response involved a search and rescue operation focusing on the South China Sea. As more information emerged, the search area expanded to the Strait of Malacca and the Andaman Sea. The initial search involved numerous countries, including Malaysia, China, Vietnam, and the United States, deploying ships, aircraft, and satellites. However, despite these efforts, no trace of the aircraft was found in the initial search areas.

The investigation took a significant turn when analysis of satellite communications revealed that the aircraft continued to fly for several hours after losing contact with air traffic control. Inmarsat, the British satellite telecommunications company, provided crucial data from its network, showing that Flight MH370 continued to send automated hourly 'handshakes' to one of its satellites. By analyzing these 'handshakes,' investigators determined that the aircraft flew southward over the Indian Ocean. This information significantly shifted the focus of the search to a remote area of the southern Indian Ocean, far from any possible landing sites.

The new search area, approximately 1,200 miles southwest of Perth, Australia, presented significant challenges. The southern Indian Ocean is one of the most isolated and deep ocean regions in the world, with depths reaching up to 23,000 feet and subject to extreme weather conditions. Despite these challenges, an extensive underwater search commenced, led by the Australian Transport Safety Bureau (ATSB), with assistance from numerous international organizations and experts.

The underwater search involved the use of advanced technology, including sonar-equipped ships and autonomous underwater vehicles (AUVs) capable of mapping the ocean floor. The search area, determined based on the satellite data and further analysis by experts in ocean drift and flight dynamics, covered approximately 120,000 square kilometers. Despite the comprehensive nature of this search, it failed to locate the wreckage of MH370.

In 2015, over a year after the disappearance, a piece of aircraft debris known as a flaperon was found on the shores of Réunion Island in the Indian Ocean. The flaperon was confirmed to be from MH370, providing the first physical evidence that the aircraft had indeed crashed into the Indian Ocean. Subsequent searches along the coastlines of the western Indian Ocean turned up additional debris, including interior panels and other parts consistent with a Boeing 777.

These discoveries, while significant, did not provide enough evidence to determine the exact location of the main wreckage or to understand the circumstances leading to the crash. Theories about the disappearance of MH370 abound, ranging from catastrophic mechanical failure and hijacking to more complex scenarios involving deliberate actions by one of the pilots. However, without the flight data recorder (FDR) and cockpit voice recorder (CVR), which are presumed to be on the ocean floor, the exact cause of the disappearance remains unknown.

Several independent investigations and analyses have been conducted in addition to the official investigation. For instance, a report by the Australian Transport Safety Bureau in 2017 emphasized the likelihood of a high-speed dive into the ocean, consistent with the flaperon's condition. The report suggested that the aircraft was not configured for a controlled ditching, implying that it may have run out of fuel and plunged rapidly into the sea.

Another significant theory involves the possibility of a deliberate act by Captain Zaharie Ahmad Shah. Some investigators believe that the aircraft's complex flight path, particularly the turn back over the Malay Peninsula, could indicate that someone with considerable flying experience was in control. Investigations into Zaharie's background revealed a home flight simulator with routes resembling the flight's path, though this evidence is not conclusive and remains highly debated.

In January 2018, a private company, Ocean Infinity, undertook a new search for MH370, operating under a "no find, no fee" arrangement with the Malaysian government. Using state-of-the-art AUVs capable of scanning large areas of the ocean floor, Ocean Infinity covered an additional 112,000 square kilometers. However, this search also ended without locating the wreckage, and the mission was concluded in May 2018.

The disappearance of MH370 has prompted widespread changes in the aviation industry aimed at preventing similar incidents. These changes include improvements in aircraft tracking, such as the adoption of the Global Aeronautical Distress and Safety System (GADSS) by the International Civil Aviation Organization (ICAO), which mandates regular position reporting and better emergency communication systems for aircraft flying over remote areas.

The tragedy of Flight MH370 has had profound effects on the families of the passengers and crew, who have struggled with the lack of closure and the uncertainties surrounding the loss of their loved ones. Various memorials and tributes have been established to honor the victims, and support groups continue to advocate for ongoing efforts to solve the mystery.

Despite exhaustive searches and extensive investigations, the disappearance of Malaysia Airlines Flight MH370 remains one of aviation's greatest mysteries. The unanswered questions about what happened in the final hours of the flight continue to captivate and confound experts, investigators, and the general public. The quest for answers endures, driven by a combination of technological advances, scientific inquiry, and the unyielding determination of those affected by this unprecedented aviation disaster.

Chapter 3: TWA Flight 800

Trans World Airlines Flight 800 was a Boeing 747-100 that exploded and crashed into the Atlantic Ocean near East Moriches, New York, on July 17, 1996. The aircraft was en route from John F. Kennedy International Airport in New York City to Charles de Gaulle Airport in Paris, carrying 230 people on board—212 passengers and 18 crew members. All aboard perished, marking one of the deadliest aviation disasters in U.S. history. The subsequent investigation by the National Transportation Safety Board (NTSB) became one of the most complex and contentious in aviation history, spanning over four years and involving multiple theories and considerable public interest.

Flight 800 departed JFK at 8:19 p.m. Eastern Daylight Time (EDT), about 12 minutes behind schedule. The flight crew comprised Captain Ralph G. Kevorkian, First Officer Steven E. Snyder, Flight Engineer Richard G. Campbell, and Flight Engineer Trainee Oliver Krick. At approximately 8:31 p.m., just as the aircraft was climbing through 13,700 feet and transitioning from climb to cruise phase, an explosion occurred. Witnesses on the ground and in other aircraft reported seeing a bright flash and what appeared to be a fireball falling into the ocean.

Immediately after the explosion, the aircraft broke apart. The forward portion, including the cockpit and first-class section, separated from the rest of the fuselage. The main wreckage, including the center wing tank, continued to ascend briefly before disintegrating and falling into the ocean. The debris field spanned a wide area, complicating recovery efforts.

The U.S. Coast Guard and other emergency response teams were mobilized quickly, but it was clear that there were no survivors. The recovery of bodies and wreckage began almost immediately, with ships, aircraft, and submersibles employed in the effort. Over the next few weeks, the majority of the aircraft was recovered from the ocean floor, providing crucial evidence for investigators.

The NTSB, along with the Federal Bureau of Investigation (FBI), launched a comprehensive investigation to determine the cause of the disaster. The FBI's involvement was initially predicated on the possibility of a criminal act, such as terrorism or sabotage, given the nature of the explosion and the geopolitical climate of the time. However, the NTSB's primary focus was on determining whether the crash was due to a mechanical failure, human error, or other factors.

Investigators meticulously reconstructed parts of the aircraft from recovered debris, creating a partial mock-up of the fuselage. The reconstruction and analysis focused heavily on the center wing fuel tank, which was suspected to be the source of the explosion. Initial attention was given to the possibility of a missile strike, given numerous eyewitness reports of streaks of light ascending towards the aircraft before the explosion. This theory gained significant traction in the media and among the public.

The missile theory posited that Flight 800 had been brought down either by a terrorist attack or by a missile fired accidentally during a military exercise. Extensive analysis of the wreckage, radar data, and interviews with witnesses were conducted to investigate these claims. Additionally, the FBI and other agencies conducted thorough reviews of all available intelligence and military activity in the area on the night of the disaster.

Despite the missile theory's prominence, no definitive evidence was found to support it. Radar data did not indicate the presence of any missile tracks, and no missile debris was recovered from the ocean. The FBI eventually concluded its investigation without finding any evidence of a criminal act, turning the focus back to a mechanical failure.

The NTSB's investigation revealed that the most likely cause of the explosion was a fuel-air mixture in the center wing tank that ignited.

The 747 had departed with a relatively low fuel load, and the center wing tank contained only a small amount of fuel, primarily vapors. The weather in New York City had been hot and humid, causing the fuel vapors to become more volatile. The NTSB determined that a short circuit outside the tank caused high voltage to enter the fuel quantity indication system wiring, which ignited the flammable fuel/air mixture in the tank.

The exact source of the ignition could not be pinpointed, but the investigation highlighted several potential ignition points. Among them were damaged wires, known as "arc tracking," and compromised insulation. The investigation also noted that maintenance practices and the aging condition of the aircraft's wiring could have contributed to the conditions that led to the short circuit.

On August 23, 2000, the NTSB issued its final report, concluding that the probable cause of the TWA Flight 800 disaster was an explosion of the center wing fuel tank resulting from the ignition of a flammable fuel/air mixture, most likely due to a short circuit. The report included several safety recommendations aimed at preventing similar incidents in the future, focusing on reducing the likelihood of ignition sources within fuel tanks and improving the safety and maintenance of electrical wiring on aircraft.

One of the significant recommendations was the implementation of nitrogen inerting systems for fuel tanks. These systems reduce the risk of explosions by displacing oxygen with nitrogen, thus preventing the formation of a flammable mixture. The Federal Aviation Administration (FAA) mandated the introduction of such systems in new aircraft and retrofitting existing ones to enhance safety.

The TWA Flight 800 disaster had a profound impact on aviation safety and the procedures for investigating air accidents. It underscored the importance of rigorous maintenance practices and the need for continuous monitoring of aging aircraft. The extensive and contentious nature of the investigation also highlighted the challenges faced by investigative bodies in balancing thorough technical analysis with addressing public and media scrutiny.

For the families of the victims, the lengthy investigation provided some answers but also extended the period of uncertainty and grief. Memorials were established, including a permanent memorial at Smith Point County Park in Long Island, near the crash site, to honor the victims and provide a place of remembrance for their families and the public.

The TWA Flight 800 tragedy remains a pivotal case study in aviation safety and accident investigation, illustrating the complexities and interdependencies of modern aircraft systems. While the exact ignition source may never be determined with absolute certainty, the lessons learned have contributed to significant advancements in preventing similar catastrophes, reinforcing the ongoing commitment to aviation safety and the prevention of future tragedies.

Chapter 4: Air France Flight 447

Air France Flight 447 was a scheduled international passenger flight from Rio de Janeiro, Brazil, to Paris, France. On June 1, 2009, the Airbus A330-203 aircraft operating the flight crashed into the Atlantic Ocean, killing all 228 passengers and crew on board. The crash and subsequent investigation highlighted significant issues in aviation safety, pilot training, and the interaction between human operators and automated systems. The disaster became one of the deadliest in the history of aviation and a profound case study in the complexities of modern flight operations.

Flight 447 departed from Rio de Janeiro-Galeão International Airport at 7:29 p.m. local time on May 31, 2009. The aircraft, registered as F-GZCP, was under the command of Captain Marc Dubois, with First Officer David Robert and First Officer Pierre-Cédric Bonin serving as co-pilots. The flight plan took the aircraft over the Atlantic Ocean, where it was scheduled to enter French airspace before landing at Paris-Charles de Gaulle Airport.

As the aircraft approached its cruising altitude of 35,000 feet, the flight was uneventful, with no indications of technical problems. However, the flight path took the aircraft through an area known for severe weather conditions, the Intertropical Convergence Zone (ITCZ), characterized by thunderstorms and heavy turbulence. At approximately 11:00 p.m. UTC, the crew received a weather briefing indicating potential turbulence ahead. The flight crew adjusted the flight path slightly to avoid the most severe weather, but they could not completely bypass the turbulent area.

At 2:10 a.m. UTC, the flight entered a storm system, and the aircraft experienced moderate turbulence. The pitot tubes, which measure airspeed, began to ice over. This caused inconsistencies in the airspeed readings sent to the flight control computers. At 2:11 a.m., the autopilot and autothrust systems disengaged, reverting the aircraft to "alternate law" flight mode, which provides fewer protections against pilot errors than the normal flight mode.

With the autopilot disengaged, First Officer Bonin, who was the pilot flying at the time, took manual control of the aircraft. Confused by the conflicting airspeed readings and the loss of automated systems, Bonin made a series of control inputs that caused the aircraft to climb steeply. The aircraft's angle of attack increased dramatically, leading to an aerodynamic stall. Despite the aircraft's stall warning system activating, Bonin continued to pull back on the control stick, exacerbating the situation.

As the aircraft entered the stall, the flight crew struggled to understand what was happening. The stall warning sounded repeatedly, but the crew did not recognize the situation for what it was. The confusion was compounded by the loss of reliable airspeed data and the stressful conditions of flying manually in turbulent weather at night. Captain Dubois, who had been taking a rest break, returned to the cockpit at this point but was unable to regain control of the aircraft in time.

For the next three and a half minutes, the aircraft descended rapidly from its cruising altitude, falling at a rate of 10,000 feet per minute. The flight crew made increasingly desperate attempts to regain control, but the aircraft remained stalled. At 2:14 a.m. UTC, the aircraft struck the ocean surface at a high rate of descent and a forward speed of 107 knots, breaking apart on impact and killing everyone on board instantly.

The search for the wreckage of Flight 447 was one of the most challenging and extensive in aviation history. Initial searches were hampered by the remote location of the crash site, deep ocean waters, and adverse weather conditions. The first phase of the search, conducted by the French Navy and international partners, focused on locating floating debris and bodies. Within days, debris and bodies were recovered from the ocean, confirming the worst fears.

However, the critical components needed for the investigation, such as the flight data recorder (FDR) and the cockpit voice recorder (CVR), remained elusive. These devices, essential for understanding the sequence of events leading to the crash, were located on the ocean floor, at depths of up to 13,000 feet. Multiple search efforts over the following months and years employed advanced technology, including deep-sea submersibles and sonar mapping, but were initially unsuccessful.

It was not until April 2011, nearly two years after the crash, that the FDR and CVR were finally located and recovered by a specialized underwater search team. The data retrieved from these recorders provided crucial insights into the final moments of Flight 447 and the chain of events that led to the disaster.

The investigation, led by the French Bureau of Enquiry and Analysis for Civil Aviation Safety (BEA), concluded that the primary cause of the crash was the flight crew's failure to respond appropriately to the aircraft's stall. The BEA's final report, released in July 2012, identified several contributing factors, including:

1. **Pitot Tube Icing**: The icing over of the pitot tubes led to the loss of reliable airspeed data, causing the autopilot and autothrust systems to disengage. This situation required the pilots to fly the aircraft manually, a scenario for which they were not adequately prepared.

2. **Pilot Training and Experience**: The report highlighted deficiencies in the pilots' training, particularly in recognizing and recovering from a high-altitude aerodynamic stall. The pilots had limited experience flying manually at cruise altitude and were not sufficiently trained to handle the situation that arose.

3. **Crew Coordination and Communication**: The investigation revealed issues with crew resource management (CRM). The

communication and coordination among the flight crew during the crisis were inadequate, leading to confusion and a lack of effective response to the emergency.

4. **Human-Machine Interface**: The design of the aircraft's automated systems and the way they interacted with the pilots were also scrutinized. The transition from automated to manual flight was abrupt, and the available information did not adequately support the pilots in diagnosing the problem and taking corrective action.

5. **Operational and Organizational Factors**: The investigation also examined Air France's operational procedures and organizational culture. Recommendations were made to improve pilot training programs, particularly in handling abnormal situations and enhancing CRM.

The crash of Air France Flight 447 had a profound impact on the aviation industry, prompting significant changes in training, procedures, and technology. One of the major outcomes was the increased emphasis on upset recovery training for pilots. Airlines and aviation authorities around the world updated their training programs to ensure that pilots were better prepared to handle unusual attitudes and aerodynamic stalls.

Additionally, the crash underscored the importance of reliable airspeed indication systems. Manufacturers and regulators introduced improvements to pitot tube design and maintenance to reduce the likelihood of similar icing incidents. The International Civil Aviation Organization (ICAO) and other regulatory bodies also reviewed and updated their standards for aircraft design and operations.

The tragedy of Flight 447 also brought attention to the psychological and physiological aspects of pilot performance under stress. Research and training programs have since focused more on understanding how pilots react in high-stress situations and how training can be enhanced to improve decision-making and performance under pressure.

For the families of the victims, the crash of Flight 447 was a devastating loss. Memorials were established in France and Brazil, and the French government held ceremonies to honor the memory of those who perished. The extended search and investigation, while providing some answers, also prolonged the grief and uncertainty for many of the families involved.

The lessons learned from the investigation into Air France Flight 447 continue to resonate within the aviation community. The disaster highlighted the critical importance of continuous improvement in training, technology, and procedures to enhance safety. It also underscored the need for effective communication and coordination among flight crews, particularly in emergency situations.

While the crash of Air France Flight 447 remains a tragic chapter in aviation history, the advancements made in its aftermath have contributed to making air travel safer for millions of passengers worldwide. The ongoing commitment to learning from such incidents and implementing changes to prevent future tragedies is a testament to the resilience and dedication of the global aviation community.

Chapter 5: Korean Air Lines Flight 007

Korean Air Lines Flight 007 (KAL 007) was a scheduled flight from New York City to Seoul via Anchorage that was shot down by a Soviet Su-15 interceptor on September 1, 1983. The incident occurred after the Boeing 747-230B aircraft strayed into prohibited Soviet airspace, leading to the loss of all 269 passengers and crew on board. This event marked a significant and controversial episode during the Cold War, highlighting the tensions between the United States and the Soviet Union and raising critical questions about aviation navigation, military protocols, and international diplomacy.

Flight 007 took off from John F. Kennedy International Airport in New York City on August 31, 1983, bound for Seoul, South Korea, with a planned refueling stop in Anchorage, Alaska. The aircraft was piloted by Captain Chun Byung-in, an experienced aviator with nearly 11,000 flight hours, and First Officer Son Dong-hui, with almost 9,000 flight hours. Also in the cockpit was Flight Engineer Kim Eui-dong. The aircraft was carrying 240 passengers, including a mix of South Koreans, Japanese, and Americans, and 29 crew members.

After an uneventful flight from New York to Anchorage, the aircraft departed Anchorage at 4:00 AM local time on September 1, 1983. The planned flight path would have taken KAL 007 on a great circle route over the North Pacific, skirting the Kamchatka Peninsula before crossing into South Korean airspace. However, shortly after departure, the aircraft began deviating from its intended course, heading further to the north and west, eventually entering Soviet airspace.

This deviation was not immediately recognized by the flight crew, nor was it detected by the air traffic controllers in Anchorage. It is believed that the deviation occurred due to a combination of navigational errors, possibly including a failure to engage the inertial navigation system (INS) correctly. As a result, KAL 007 flew on a parallel path approximately 245 miles to the west of its intended course.

The flight continued into Soviet airspace over the Kamchatka Peninsula, an area heavily monitored due to its strategic military significance. Soviet air defense forces detected the intrusion and scrambled fighter jets to intercept the unknown aircraft. Initially, the Soviet pilots failed to locate KAL 007, and the aircraft exited Soviet airspace without incident. However, the aircraft's trajectory then led it into a second, more sensitive area of Soviet airspace over Sakhalin Island.

At this point, the Soviet Union was on high alert due to increased tensions with the United States. There were frequent reconnaissance flights by U.S. military aircraft, and the Soviets were highly sensitive to any incursions into their airspace. When KAL 007 re-entered Soviet airspace over Sakhalin, the Soviet military once again scrambled interceptors. This time, the fighters, including a Su-15 interceptor piloted by Major Gennadi Osipovich, successfully located the aircraft.

The Soviet pilots attempted to communicate with KAL 007, signaling for it to follow them and land. However, these signals were not acknowledged by the KAL 007 flight crew, likely because they did not see them or did not understand their intent. The situation escalated rapidly, and after receiving clearance from Soviet military command, Major Osipovich launched two R-98 air-to-air missiles at the aircraft.

At approximately 18:26 UTC, the missiles struck KAL 007, causing catastrophic damage. One missile exploded near the tail, and the other hit the fuselage near the left wing. The aircraft began to depressurize and lose control. Despite the damage, the aircraft remained airborne for several minutes, descending rapidly before crashing into the Sea of Japan near Moneron Island. All 269 people on board were killed.

The immediate aftermath of the incident saw a flurry of accusations and denials between the Soviet Union and the United States. The

Soviet government initially denied any knowledge of the incident, but as evidence mounted, including intercepts of Soviet military communications and satellite imagery, they admitted to shooting down the aircraft. However, they maintained that the aircraft had been on an espionage mission and that the intrusion into Soviet airspace was deliberate.

The United States and its allies condemned the attack, characterizing it as a brutal and unjustified act against a civilian airliner. President Ronald Reagan addressed the nation, denouncing the Soviet action and calling it a massacre. The incident intensified Cold War tensions and led to a series of diplomatic and economic sanctions against the Soviet Union.

The investigation into the shootdown of KAL 007 was conducted by the International Civil Aviation Organization (ICAO). The investigation was hampered by the lack of cooperation from the Soviet Union, which delayed access to key evidence, including the flight data recorder (FDR) and cockpit voice recorder (CVR). These recorders, crucial for understanding the events leading up to the crash, were only made available after the collapse of the Soviet Union in 1991.

The ICAO's final report, released in 1993, concluded that the deviation from the planned flight path was likely due to a combination of pilot error and navigational system failure. The report criticized the Soviet military's actions, noting that they had failed to positively identify the aircraft as a civilian airliner and had not exhausted all available means to communicate with the flight crew before resorting to the use of force.

The investigation also highlighted several deficiencies in international aviation protocols. One of the key recommendations was the need for improved coordination and communication between civilian air traffic control and military defense systems to prevent similar incidents in the future. Additionally, the incident underscored the importance of accurate and reliable navigational aids, leading to improvements in global navigation satellite systems and the introduction of stricter standards for flight crew training and equipment maintenance.

The downing of KAL 007 had far-reaching implications for international aviation and geopolitical relations. It prompted significant changes in air navigation systems, including the development and implementation of the Global Positioning System (GPS) for civilian use, which provided more accurate and reliable navigation for aircraft. The incident also led to the creation of special air corridors over sensitive areas to ensure that civilian aircraft did not inadvertently enter restricted airspace.

In the years following the incident, the families of the victims sought answers and accountability. Various lawsuits were filed against Korean Air Lines and the Soviet government. Korean Air Lines faced scrutiny over its flight operations and safety protocols, leading to internal reviews and changes in company policies.

Memorials were established in several countries to honor the victims of Flight 007. In South Korea, a memorial was erected in Yangjae Citizens' Forest in Seoul, while another memorial was placed in Anchorage, Alaska. These memorials serve as reminders of the tragic event and the lives lost.

The geopolitical context of the Cold War played a significant role in the incident and its aftermath. The shootdown of KAL 007 exacerbated existing tensions between the superpowers and highlighted the dangers of miscommunication and miscalculation in an era of heightened suspicion and hostility. The incident underscored the need for clearer communication channels and protocols to prevent misunderstandings and ensure the safety of civilian aviation.

In the broader context of aviation history, the downing of KAL 007 remains a poignant reminder of the complexities and risks associated with international air travel, particularly in regions with sensitive military activities. The lessons learned from this incident have contributed to ongoing efforts to improve aviation safety, enhance navigational systems, and foster better cooperation between civilian and military aviation authorities.

The tragic loss of Korean Air Lines Flight 007 continues to resonate as a symbol of the human cost of geopolitical conflict and the enduring quest for safer skies. The legacy of the incident is reflected in the advancements in aviation technology and protocols that have since been implemented to prevent such tragedies from occurring again.

Chapter 6: Pan Am Flight 103 (Lockerbie)

Pan Am Flight 103, commonly referred to as the Lockerbie bombing, was a transatlantic flight from Frankfurt, Germany, to Detroit, Michigan, via London Heathrow and New York JFK, that was destroyed by a terrorist bomb on December 21, 1988. The explosion caused the Boeing 747-121 aircraft, named Clipper Maid of the Seas, to crash into the town of Lockerbie, Scotland, killing all 259 passengers and crew on board, as well as 11 residents on the ground. The event marked one of the deadliest terrorist attacks in aviation history and led to a prolonged international investigation, significant changes in aviation security, and enduring geopolitical ramifications.

Pan Am Flight 103 departed from Frankfurt International Airport at 4:00 PM local time on December 21, 1988. The aircraft was scheduled to stop at London Heathrow Airport before crossing the Atlantic Ocean to John F. Kennedy International Airport in New York City, and then continuing to its final destination in Detroit. The flight crew was led by Captain James Bruce MacQuarrie, First Officer Raymond R. Wagner, and Flight Engineer Jerry Don Avritt. The aircraft carried 243 passengers from 21 countries and 16 crew members.

The flight's first leg to London was routine, and the aircraft landed at Heathrow at approximately 5:30 PM local time. After a layover, the plane took off for New York at 6:25 PM. At around 7:03 PM, as the aircraft was cruising at 31,000 feet over the Scottish border, a bomb hidden in a suitcase in the forward cargo hold detonated. The explosion caused rapid decompression and the breakup of the aircraft, scattering debris over an extensive area of Lockerbie and its surroundings.

The explosion and subsequent crash led to an immediate loss of life for all those aboard the aircraft. The debris from the explosion caused massive damage on the ground, striking homes and infrastructure in Lockerbie and resulting in the deaths of 11 residents. The largest piece of wreckage, including the cockpit and forward fuselage, landed on Sherwood Crescent, causing a large crater and fire that destroyed several houses.

The initial response to the disaster involved emergency services from Scotland and the UK, who faced the grim task of recovering bodies and securing the extensive debris field. The Royal Air Force (RAF), local police, and other agencies collaborated in the recovery efforts. In the days following the crash, the recovery teams painstakingly gathered evidence, including parts of the aircraft, luggage, and personal belongings, to determine the cause of the explosion.

The investigation into the bombing was led by the Dumfries and Galloway Constabulary, with assistance from the FBI and Scotland Yard. Forensic experts analyzed the wreckage and quickly determined that the explosion had been caused by a bomb. Traces of the explosive PETN (Pentaerythritol tetranitrate) were found, and fragments of a timing device and a radio cassette player were identified as components of the bomb. Further investigation revealed that the explosive device had been hidden inside a Toshiba Bombeat 453 radio cassette player, which had been packed into a Samsonite suitcase.

The suitcase containing the bomb had been transferred to Pan Am Flight 103 from an Air Malta flight that had arrived in Frankfurt. This revelation led investigators to focus on the passenger and baggage handling processes at Frankfurt Airport. They discovered that the suitcase had been checked in without an accompanying passenger, a significant breach of security protocols at the time.

The investigation eventually pointed to two Libyan nationals, Abdelbaset al-Megrahi and Lamin Khalifah Fhimah, as the primary suspects. Al-Megrahi was an intelligence officer, and Fhimah was the station manager for Libyan Arab Airlines in Malta. The evidence indicated that the bomb had been placed on the Air Malta flight in Malta and then transferred to Pan Am Flight 103 in Frankfurt.

The political and diplomatic dimensions of the case were complex and fraught with tension. The Libyan government, led by Colonel Muammar Gaddafi, was accused of orchestrating the bombing as an act of revenge against the United States and the United Kingdom for their military actions against Libya. In the years leading up to the bombing, Libya had been involved in several confrontations with Western nations, including the 1986 U.S. airstrikes on Tripoli and Benghazi, which were in retaliation for the bombing of a Berlin nightclub frequented by U.S. military personnel.

The process of bringing the suspects to justice was protracted and involved extensive negotiations between Libya, the United States, and the United Kingdom. In 1991, the U.S. and UK governments formally charged al-Megrahi and Fhimah and demanded their extradition. Libya initially refused to hand over the suspects, leading to a standoff that resulted in international sanctions imposed by the United Nations.

It was not until 1999 that a breakthrough was achieved. Under considerable international pressure, Gaddafi agreed to surrender al-Megrahi and Fhimah for trial in a neutral country. The suspects were handed over to Scottish authorities and flown to the Netherlands, where they were tried under Scottish law at a specially convened court in Camp Zeist.

The trial began in May 2000 and lasted until January 2001. Fhimah was acquitted of all charges due to insufficient evidence, while al-Megrahi was found guilty of 270 counts of murder and sentenced to life imprisonment, with a minimum term of 27 years. Al-Megrahi maintained his innocence, and his conviction was the subject of ongoing legal battles and appeals.

In 2009, al-Megrahi was released on compassionate grounds by the Scottish government after being diagnosed with terminal cancer. His release sparked controversy and outrage, particularly among the families of the victims, who saw it as a miscarriage of justice. Al-Megrahi returned to Libya, where he died in 2012.

The Pan Am Flight 103 bombing had a profound impact on international aviation security. It exposed significant vulnerabilities in airport and airline security procedures, particularly regarding baggage handling and passenger screening. In response, regulatory authorities worldwide implemented stringent new security measures, including enhanced baggage screening, stricter controls on unaccompanied baggage, and improved passenger profiling techniques.

The bombing also led to the establishment of the Air Transport Security Act in the United States, which mandated comprehensive security programs for airlines and airports. The Federal Aviation Administration (FAA) and other regulatory bodies introduced measures to prevent similar attacks, such as reinforcing cockpit doors, deploying explosive detection systems, and increasing the presence of air marshals on flights.

In addition to the immediate security reforms, the Lockerbie bombing had lasting geopolitical ramifications. The incident underscored the threat posed by state-sponsored terrorism and the need for international cooperation to combat it. The United Nations imposed economic sanctions on Libya, which remained in place until 2003 when Gaddafi's government formally accepted responsibility for the bombing and agreed to compensate the families of the victims. Libya's acceptance of responsibility and renouncement of terrorism led to a normalization of relations with the West, although the legacy of the bombing continued to influence international relations.

The victims of Pan Am Flight 103 were memorialized in numerous ways. A garden of remembrance was established in Lockerbie, and a memorial cairn was erected at Arlington National Cemetery in the

United States. These memorials serve as places of reflection and commemoration for the families of the victims and the broader public.

Each year, ceremonies are held to honor the memory of those who perished, and scholarships have been established in their names. The town of Lockerbie has maintained a close relationship with Syracuse University, which lost 35 students in the bombing. The university established the Remembrance Scholarship program, which provides scholarships to students who embody the qualities of those lost in the tragedy.

The Pan Am Flight 103 bombing remains a pivotal moment in the history of aviation and counterterrorism. It highlighted the devastating impact of terrorism on innocent lives and the importance of international cooperation in ensuring the safety and security of air travel. The lessons learned from the tragedy continue to inform security practices and policies to this day, underscoring the need for vigilance and resilience in the face of evolving threats.

Chapter 7: American Airlines Flight 587

American Airlines Flight 587 was a scheduled international passenger flight from John F. Kennedy International Airport (JFK) in New York City to Las Américas International Airport in Santo Domingo, Dominican Republic. On November 12, 2001, the Airbus A300B4-605R aircraft operating the flight crashed into the Belle Harbor neighborhood of Queens, New York, shortly after takeoff. The disaster resulted in the deaths of all 260 passengers and crew on board, as well as five people on the ground. This tragic event stands as one of the deadliest aviation accidents in U.S. history and brought significant attention to issues of aircraft design, pilot training, and emergency response.

On the morning of November 12, 2001, Flight 587 was under the command of Captain Edward States and First Officer Sten Molin. Captain States, aged 42, had approximately 8,050 hours of flight experience, including over 1,100 hours on the Airbus A300. First Officer Molin, aged 34, had around 4,403 hours of flight experience, with more than 1,835 hours on the Airbus A300. The aircraft was carrying 251 passengers, most of whom were Dominican nationals traveling home or visiting family, along with nine crew members.

Flight 587 taxied to Runway 31L at JFK and received clearance for takeoff at 9:11 AM EST. The weather conditions were clear, with good visibility and light winds. The initial takeoff and climb were routine until the aircraft encountered wake turbulence from a Japan Airlines Boeing 747 that had taken off just before Flight 587. Wake turbulence consists of powerful vortices created by the wingtips of large aircraft, and it can be hazardous, particularly during takeoff and landing phases.

At approximately 9:15 AM, as Flight 587 climbed to 2,500 feet, it encountered wake turbulence from the 747. In response to the turbulence, First Officer Molin, who was the pilot flying the aircraft, made a series of control inputs to stabilize the plane. He applied several large, alternating rudder inputs, which led to excessive side-to-side movements of the aircraft's tail. The aerodynamic forces generated by these rudder inputs stressed the vertical stabilizer and the rudder beyond their design limits.

The National Transportation Safety Board (NTSB) later determined that these excessive rudder inputs caused the vertical stabilizer to separate from the fuselage. Without the vertical stabilizer, the aircraft became uncontrollable. At 9:16 AM, less than three minutes after takeoff, Flight 587 crashed into the Belle Harbor neighborhood in Queens. The impact destroyed several homes and caused a massive fire, devastating the residential area.

The immediate aftermath of the crash was chaotic and tragic. Emergency responders, including firefighters, police, and medical personnel, quickly arrived at the scene, but there was little they could do to save lives, as the crash had been catastrophic. The fire took hours to bring under control, and the debris was scattered over a wide area, complicating recovery efforts. The crash site in Belle Harbor, a close-knit community still reeling from the September 11 attacks just two months earlier, was left in shock and grief.

The NTSB launched a comprehensive investigation to determine the cause of the accident. The investigation included analyzing the flight data recorder (FDR) and cockpit voice recorder (CVR), examining the wreckage, and conducting simulations of the flight conditions. The NTSB's final report, released in October 2004, identified several key factors contributing to the crash.

The primary cause of the crash was determined to be the inappropriate rudder inputs made by First Officer Molin in response to the wake turbulence. The NTSB found that Molin's training may not have adequately prepared him to handle such turbulence without overreacting. The alternating rudder inputs led to aerodynamic forces that exceeded the design limits of the vertical stabilizer, resulting in its separation from the aircraft.

The investigation also highlighted issues related to the Airbus A300's rudder control system and its sensitivity to pilot inputs. The A300's rudder system allowed for large movements with relatively small pedal inputs, making it easier for pilots to unintentionally exert excessive forces on the aircraft's structure. The NTSB recommended that Airbus and other aircraft manufacturers review and modify their rudder control systems to prevent similar incidents.

Additionally, the NTSB emphasized the importance of enhanced pilot training programs to address the handling of wake turbulence and the appropriate use of rudder inputs. It recommended that airlines incorporate simulator training scenarios involving wake turbulence encounters and rudder control to ensure pilots are better prepared for such situations.

The crash of Flight 587 also raised concerns about emergency response and disaster management in urban settings. The immediate response by New York City's emergency services was swift, but the scale of the disaster highlighted the challenges of coordinating efforts in densely populated areas. The incident underscored the need for ongoing training and preparedness for large-scale emergencies, particularly in cities with significant air traffic.

In the years following the crash, American Airlines and other carriers implemented changes to their pilot training programs to address the issues identified by the NTSB. These changes included enhanced simulator training for wake turbulence encounters, better education on the appropriate use of rudder controls, and increased emphasis on cockpit resource management (CRM) to ensure effective communication and decision-making during flight.

The aircraft's manufacturer, Airbus, also took steps to address the findings of the NTSB investigation. Modifications were made to the rudder control system on the A300 and other models to reduce the risk of excessive forces being applied. Airbus worked with regulatory authorities to update design standards and operating procedures to enhance safety.

For the families of the victims, the crash of Flight 587 was a devastating loss. Memorial services were held in New York and the Dominican Republic, and a permanent memorial was established in Belle Harbor to honor those who perished. The memorial, located in Rockaway Park, Queens, features a curved wall inscribed with the names of the victims and serves as a place of reflection and remembrance.

The crash also had a significant impact on the Dominican community in New York City, which lost many of its members in the disaster. The event brought the community together in grief and solidarity, and various support groups and organizations were established to provide assistance to the families affected by the tragedy.

In the broader context of aviation safety, the crash of American Airlines Flight 587 prompted ongoing efforts to improve pilot training, aircraft design, and emergency response protocols. The lessons learned from the incident have contributed to advancements in understanding the dynamics of wake turbulence, the importance of appropriate pilot responses, and the need for continuous improvement in aviation safety standards.

The legacy of Flight 587 is a testament to the resilience of the aviation industry and the determination to learn from tragedies to prevent future accidents. The improvements in training, technology, and safety procedures that followed the crash have helped enhance the safety of air travel for millions of passengers worldwide. The memory of those who lost their lives in the disaster continues to inspire efforts to ensure that such a tragedy is never repeated.

Chapter 8: Air India Flight 182

Air India Flight 182 was a scheduled passenger flight operating from Montreal, Canada, to New Delhi, India, with a stopover in London, United Kingdom. On June 23, 1985, the Boeing 747-237B aircraft, named Emperor Kanishka, was destroyed by a bomb at an altitude of 31,000 feet (9,400 meters) off the coast of Ireland. All 329 people on board were killed, making it one of the deadliest aviation disasters in history and the worst act of aviation terrorism before the September 11 attacks in 2001. The bombing of Air India Flight 182 was a tragic culmination of a series of events driven by political and religious conflicts, resulting in a long and complex investigation that exposed significant failures in security and intelligence.

The story of Air India Flight 182 begins against the backdrop of the rising tensions between Sikh separatists and the Indian government during the 1980s. The demand for an independent Sikh state, Khalistan, led to increased militancy among certain factions of the Sikh community. In June 1984, the Indian government launched Operation Blue Star, a military operation aimed at removing armed militants from the Golden Temple in Amritsar, the holiest site in Sikhism. The operation resulted in significant casualties and desecration of the temple, leading to widespread outrage among Sikhs both in India and abroad.

In retaliation for Operation Blue Star, Prime Minister Indira Gandhi was assassinated by her Sikh bodyguards on October 31, 1984. This event triggered anti-Sikh riots across India, leading to further polarization and radicalization within the Sikh community. Among the radical elements, a group of Sikh militants based in Canada, led by Talwinder Singh Parmar and Inderjit Singh Reyat, began planning acts of terrorism against Indian targets.

By early 1985, Canadian authorities had received intelligence indicating a possible threat to Air India flights, but the information was not sufficiently specific, and security measures were not adequately heightened. On June 22, 1985, two pieces of luggage containing bombs were checked in at Vancouver International Airport by militants under false names. One of these bombs was destined for Air India Flight 182, while the other was placed on a connecting Canadian Pacific Airlines flight to Tokyo, where it was intended to be transferred to another Air India flight.

On the evening of June 22, Air India Flight 182 departed from Toronto Pearson International Airport, making a stop in Montreal before continuing its journey across the Atlantic. The flight carried 307 passengers, most of whom were of Indian descent, and 22 crew members. As the flight progressed, the bomb, concealed in a suitcase in the forward cargo hold, detonated at 7:14 AM GMT on June 23, 1985, over the Atlantic Ocean near the southwest coast of Ireland.

The explosion caused the aircraft to break apart mid-air, and the wreckage fell into the sea, leaving no survivors. The subsequent investigation, led by the Canadian Aviation Safety Board (CASB) and other international authorities, faced significant challenges due to the extent of the damage and the depth at which much of the wreckage lay. The primary goal of the investigation was to determine the cause of the explosion and identify those responsible for the bombing.

The initial recovery efforts focused on retrieving debris and bodies from the ocean. The Royal Navy and Irish Naval Service conducted extensive search and recovery operations, recovering bodies, personal belongings, and pieces of the aircraft. The black boxes, including the cockpit voice recorder (CVR) and flight data recorder (FDR), were eventually located and recovered from the seabed, providing crucial information for the investigation.

Analysis of the wreckage and data from the black boxes confirmed that the aircraft had been destroyed by a bomb. Traces of the explosive RDX were found, and forensic examination of the suitcase fragments pointed to the use of a timing device. The investigation then turned towards identifying the individuals responsible for planting the bomb.

Canadian law enforcement agencies, including the Royal Canadian Mounted Police (RCMP) and the Canadian Security Intelligence Service (CSIS), conducted extensive investigations into the Sikh militant groups operating in Canada. Talwinder Singh Parmar and Inderjit Singh Reyat emerged as key suspects. Parmar, the leader of the Babbar Khalsa, a militant Sikh organization, was believed to be the mastermind behind the bombing, while Reyat, an electrician by trade, was implicated in the construction of the bombs.

Despite the significant evidence pointing towards Parmar and Reyat, the investigation faced numerous obstacles, including jurisdictional issues, the destruction of crucial evidence, and challenges in securing cooperation from witnesses. Parmar was arrested in Germany shortly after the bombing but was released due to lack of evidence. He was later killed by Indian police in 1992 under murky circumstances, further complicating the pursuit of justice.

Inderjit Singh Reyat was arrested and charged in Canada. In 1991, he was convicted of manslaughter and explosives charges related to the bombing of the Canadian Pacific Airlines flight in Tokyo, which killed two baggage handlers. The prosecution's case against Reyat for his involvement in the Air India bombing took longer to build. In 2003, Reyat pled guilty to manslaughter and admitted to constructing the bomb used in Flight 182. He was sentenced to five years in prison.

The pursuit of justice for the victims of Air India Flight 182 extended beyond Reyat's conviction. In 2000, two additional suspects, Ripudaman Singh Malik and Ajaib Singh Bagri, were arrested and charged with conspiracy and murder in connection with the bombing. Their trial, one of the longest and most expensive in Canadian history, concluded in 2005 with both men being acquitted due to insufficient evidence. The acquittals were a significant setback for the families of the victims, who had waited two decades for justice.

The bombing of Air India Flight 182 exposed significant flaws in security and intelligence practices in Canada and internationally. Prior to the bombing, Canadian authorities had received warnings about potential terrorist attacks against Air India but had failed to implement adequate security measures. The intelligence-sharing and coordination between agencies such as CSIS and the RCMP were found to be inadequate, contributing to the failure to prevent the attack.

In the aftermath of the bombing, the Canadian government conducted several reviews and inquiries to address the systemic issues that had allowed the tragedy to occur. The most comprehensive of these was the Air India Inquiry, led by former Supreme Court Justice John Major, which began in 2006 and released its final report in 2010. The inquiry's findings were damning, highlighting numerous lapses in security, intelligence, and law enforcement practices.

The Major Report made several key recommendations to improve Canada's national security framework. These included enhancing the coordination and information-sharing between intelligence and law enforcement agencies, strengthening aviation security measures, improving support for victims' families, and addressing the systemic issues within Canada's multicultural policies that had allowed extremist elements to flourish.

The report also emphasized the need for accountability and transparency in national security operations. It called for the establishment of an independent body to oversee the activities of intelligence agencies and ensure that they operated within the bounds of the law while effectively addressing threats to national security.

The bombing of Air India Flight 182 had a profound impact on the affected families, many of whom lost multiple loved ones in the tragedy. The emotional and psychological toll of the disaster was immense, and the long wait for justice compounded their grief. In response to the victims' needs, the Canadian government implemented measures to provide financial compensation and support services to the families.

Memorials were established in Canada, India, and Ireland to honor the victims of Flight 182. These include the Air India Memorial in Toronto, which features a sundial with the names of the victims inscribed on it, and the Air India Memorial in Ahakista, Ireland, near the crash site, which consists of a garden and a stone monument. These memorials serve as places of reflection and remembrance for the victims' families and the broader community.

The legacy of Air India Flight 182 extends beyond the immediate aftermath of the tragedy. The bombing highlighted the global nature of terrorism and the need for international cooperation to combat it effectively. The lessons learned from the disaster have influenced security and intelligence practices worldwide, contributing to the development of more robust measures to protect aviation and prevent terrorist attacks.

In the years since the bombing, advances in aviation security have included the implementation of more sophisticated screening technologies, the introduction of stringent baggage handling procedures, and the adoption of comprehensive passenger profiling systems. These measures aim to identify and mitigate potential threats before they can cause harm, enhancing the safety of air travel for millions of passengers each year.

The story of Air India Flight 182 is a reminder of the devastating impact of terrorism on innocent lives and the importance of vigilance, accountability, and justice in the face of such threats. The tragedy underscores the need for continuous improvement in security practices, the importance of supporting victims and their families, and the necessity of addressing the underlying causes of extremism to prevent future acts of violence. The memory of those who perished on Flight 182 continues to inspire efforts to create a safer, more just world for all.

Chapter 9: Ethiopian Airlines Flight 302

Ethiopian Airlines Flight 302 was a scheduled international passenger flight from Addis Ababa Bole International Airport in Ethiopia to Jomo Kenyatta International Airport in Nairobi, Kenya. On March 10, 2019, the Boeing 737 MAX 8 aircraft operating the flight crashed near the town of Bishoftu, approximately six minutes after takeoff. Tragically, all 157 passengers and crew on board were killed. This disaster was the second fatal accident involving a Boeing 737 MAX aircraft in less than five months, following the crash of Lion Air Flight 610 in October 2018. The investigation into Ethiopian Airlines Flight 302's crash led to the worldwide grounding of the Boeing 737 MAX fleet and revealed significant issues with the aircraft's design, certification, and regulatory oversight.

Ethiopian Airlines Flight 302 departed from Addis Ababa Bole International Airport at 8:38 AM local time on March 10, 2019. The aircraft, a relatively new Boeing 737 MAX 8, had been delivered to Ethiopian Airlines in November 2018. The flight was under the command of Captain Yared Getachew, a seasoned pilot with over 8,100 flight hours, and First Officer Ahmed Nur Mohammed, who had accumulated around 350 flight hours. The flight carried 149 passengers from 35 different countries and eight crew members.

Shortly after takeoff, the flight crew reported experiencing issues with the aircraft's flight control systems. The aircraft's angle of attack (AOA) sensors, which measure the angle between the wing and the oncoming air, began transmitting erroneous data. This triggered the Maneuvering Characteristics Augmentation System (MCAS), an automated safety feature designed to prevent the aircraft from stalling. The MCAS system repeatedly forced the aircraft's nose down, despite the pilots' efforts to counteract it by pulling back on the control column.

The flight crew made a distress call to air traffic control, requesting to return to the airport due to flight control problems. Despite their efforts to stabilize the aircraft, they were unable to regain control. At approximately 8:44 AM, six minutes after takeoff, the aircraft crashed into a field near the town of Bishoftu, killing all 157 people on board. The crash site was scattered with debris, and the impact created a large crater.

The immediate response to the crash involved search and rescue operations by Ethiopian authorities, along with assistance from international experts. The Ethiopian Civil Aviation Authority (ECAA) led the investigation, with support from the United States National Transportation Safety Board (NTSB), the Federal Aviation Administration (FAA), and Boeing. The recovery of the aircraft's black boxes, including the cockpit voice recorder (CVR) and flight data recorder (FDR), was crucial in understanding the events leading up to the crash.

The preliminary investigation focused on the role of the MCAS system, which had also been implicated in the crash of Lion Air Flight 610. The MCAS system was introduced in the Boeing 737 MAX to counteract changes in the aircraft's aerodynamics due to its larger engines, which were positioned further forward on the wing compared to previous 737 models. MCAS was designed to activate based on data from the AOA sensors and automatically adjust the aircraft's pitch to prevent a stall.

In both the Ethiopian Airlines and Lion Air crashes, erroneous AOA data triggered the MCAS system, causing repeated nose-down commands that the pilots struggled to counteract. The investigation revealed that the MCAS system had several critical flaws. It relied on input from a single AOA sensor, making it vulnerable to sensor malfunctions. Additionally, the system's repeated activations made it difficult for pilots to regain control of the aircraft, especially in situations where they were not fully aware of the MCAS system's operation.

The investigation also highlighted deficiencies in the certification process of the Boeing 737 MAX by the FAA. The FAA had delegated significant portions of the certification process to Boeing, which resulted in insufficient oversight and scrutiny of the MCAS system's design and implementation. The MCAS system's potential hazards were not adequately communicated to airlines and pilots, contributing to the lack of preparedness to handle the system's malfunctions.

As a result of the Ethiopian Airlines Flight 302 crash and the preceding Lion Air crash, aviation authorities worldwide grounded the Boeing 737 MAX fleet in March 2019. The grounding affected thousands of flights and disrupted operations for airlines that operated the 737 MAX. The crisis led to a comprehensive review of the aircraft's design, software, and certification procedures.

Boeing undertook significant efforts to address the issues identified in the investigations. The company redesigned the MCAS system to take input from both AOA sensors, reducing the risk of erroneous activations. The updated system also limited the number of times MCAS could activate and allowed pilots to override the system more easily. Boeing conducted extensive testing and certification flights to ensure the safety of the redesigned system.

In addition to technical fixes, the crisis prompted a reevaluation of the regulatory framework for aircraft certification. The FAA and other international regulatory bodies faced criticism for their oversight processes and their reliance on manufacturers for self-certification. The crisis underscored the need for stronger regulatory independence, enhanced oversight, and improved communication between manufacturers, regulators, and airlines.

The grounding of the 737 MAX lasted for nearly 20 months. In November 2020, the FAA officially cleared the aircraft to return to service, subject to a series of required modifications and pilot training updates. Other international aviation authorities, including the European Union Aviation Safety Agency (EASA) and Transport Canada, conducted their own reviews before allowing the 737 MAX to resume operations in their respective jurisdictions.

The impact of the Ethiopian Airlines Flight 302 crash extended beyond the technical and regulatory realms. The tragedy deeply affected the families of the victims, who sought accountability and justice for their loved ones. The emotional and psychological toll of the disaster was immense, with families mourning the loss of parents, children, and friends. Several lawsuits were filed against Boeing, alleging negligence and seeking compensation for the victims' families.

Boeing faced significant financial and reputational damage as a result of the crisis. The company reported substantial losses due to the grounding of the 737 MAX, the suspension of deliveries, and the costs associated with redesigning the MCAS system and compensating airlines. The crisis led to leadership changes at Boeing, including the resignation of CEO Dennis Muilenburg in December 2019.

The Ethiopian Airlines Flight 302 disaster also brought attention to the importance of corporate responsibility and ethical conduct in the aviation industry. Boeing's handling of the crisis, including its initial response and communication with stakeholders, faced criticism for lacking transparency and accountability. The crisis highlighted the need for manufacturers to prioritize safety and integrity over commercial interests.

The legacy of Ethiopian Airlines Flight 302 is a sobering reminder of the critical importance of safety in aviation. The tragedy underscored the need for robust design, rigorous testing, and effective regulatory oversight to ensure the safety of aircraft and the traveling public. The lessons learned from the disaster have influenced changes in aircraft certification processes, pilot training programs, and corporate governance practices within the aviation industry.

The victims of Ethiopian Airlines Flight 302 are remembered through various memorials and initiatives aimed at honoring their memory and preventing future tragedies. In Ethiopia, a memorial was established near the crash site, and in several other countries, commemorative events were held to pay tribute to the victims. The disaster has also inspired efforts to improve aviation safety and support for the families affected by such tragedies.

Chapter 10: Lion Air Flight 610

Lion Air Flight 610 was a scheduled domestic flight from Soekarno-Hatta International Airport in Jakarta to Depati Amir Airport in Pangkal Pinang, Indonesia. On October 29, 2018, the Boeing 737 MAX 8 operating this flight tragically crashed into the Java Sea 13 minutes after takeoff, killing all 189 passengers and crew on board. This incident marked the first major accident involving the Boeing 737 MAX and set off a chain of events that would lead to the aircraft being grounded worldwide.

The flight departed from Jakarta at 6:20 AM local time. Shortly after takeoff, the pilots began experiencing serious control problems. The aircraft's nose was pitching down despite their attempts to keep it level. The pilots fought to maintain control, but the plane repeatedly entered into a dive. These erratic movements were due to the aircraft's Maneuvering Characteristics Augmentation System (MCAS), a new software installed on the 737 MAX to prevent stalls by automatically adjusting the stabilizer trim to push the nose down.

The MCAS was triggered by erroneous data from a single angle of attack (AOA) sensor, which was providing incorrect readings. This sensor had been replaced the day before after a previous flight had experienced similar issues. However, the replacement sensor was faulty, and the maintenance personnel had not identified this during their checks. The MCAS system, relying on this faulty sensor data, mistakenly believed the aircraft was in danger of stalling and continuously commanded nose-down inputs.

The pilots of Flight 610 were not adequately informed about the existence of MCAS and its behavior. The aircraft's manual did not fully explain how to handle MCAS-related anomalies. As the pilots struggled to understand what was happening, they followed standard procedures to counteract the nose-down inputs, including manual control inputs and adjustments to the trim system. However, the

MCAS would re-engage every 10 seconds, overpowering their efforts and pushing the nose down again. The constant battle with the MCAS and the lack of clear information added to the confusion and stress in the cockpit.

Compounding the problem, the pilots did not follow the runaway stabilizer checklist, which involves cutting off power to the stabilizer trim system. This crucial step could have disabled the MCAS and allowed them to regain control. Investigations later revealed that this oversight might have been due to a lack of proper training and insufficient understanding of the new system.

The flight data recorder and cockpit voice recorder were recovered from the crash site, providing vital information for investigators. The data showed that the pilots were dealing with an uncommanded nose-down trim situation almost immediately after takeoff and had attempted various corrective measures. The cockpit voice recorder captured the escalating urgency and confusion as they tried to diagnose and resolve the issue.

In the aftermath of the crash, investigations were conducted by the Indonesian National Transportation Safety Committee (NTSC), the U.S. National Transportation Safety Board (NTSB), and other international aviation authorities. The final report, released in October 2019, identified several critical factors contributing to the disaster. These included the faulty AOA sensor, inadequate pilot training on MCAS, insufficient documentation and information provided by Boeing, and lapses in maintenance procedures.

The Lion Air Flight 610 crash had profound repercussions for Boeing and the aviation industry as a whole. It exposed significant flaws in the design and certification process of the 737 MAX. The MCAS was designed to operate based on input from a single AOA sensor, making it vulnerable to sensor failures. The decision not to fully disclose the existence and functioning of MCAS to airlines and pilots was heavily criticized.

Following the Lion Air disaster, another 737 MAX crash occurred in March 2019 involving Ethiopian Airlines Flight 302, which further underscored the systemic issues with the aircraft. This second crash led to the worldwide grounding of the entire 737 MAX fleet, halting deliveries and prompting a comprehensive review of the aircraft's design and certification.

Boeing faced intense scrutiny and pressure to rectify the identified issues. The company worked on software updates to the MCAS system, adding redundancy by incorporating data from multiple AOA sensors and improving the system's logic to prevent erroneous activation. Boeing also implemented changes in pilot training programs to ensure that flight crews were adequately prepared to handle MCAS-related scenarios.

The grounding of the 737 MAX lasted for over a year, during which extensive testing and re-certification processes were carried out by aviation authorities globally. The Federal Aviation Administration (FAA) and other regulatory bodies conducted rigorous evaluations to ensure the aircraft met all safety standards before it was allowed to return to service.

The Lion Air Flight 610 tragedy highlighted the critical importance of robust safety measures, thorough pilot training, and transparent communication between aircraft manufacturers and operators. It underscored the need for the aviation industry to continuously evolve and address potential vulnerabilities in aircraft design and operation. The lessons learned from this disaster have driven significant changes in how new aircraft systems are developed, tested, and integrated into commercial aviation, with the ultimate goal of enhancing the safety and reliability of air travel for passengers worldwide.

Chapter 11: Germanwings Flight 9525

Germanwings Flight 9525 was a scheduled international passenger flight from Barcelona-El Prat Airport in Spain to Düsseldorf Airport in Germany, operated by Germanwings, a low-cost airline owned by Lufthansa. On March 24, 2015, the Airbus A320-211 aircraft crashed into the French Alps, killing all 150 passengers and crew members on board. The crash was later determined to be a deliberate act by the co-pilot, Andreas Lubitz, making it one of the most tragic and shocking events in aviation history.

The aircraft departed Barcelona at 10:01 AM local time, climbing to its cruising altitude of 38,000 feet. The flight proceeded uneventfully for the first 30 minutes. At 10:27 AM, the captain, Patrick Sondenheimer, handed control of the aircraft to the co-pilot, Andreas Lubitz, and left the cockpit, presumably to use the lavatory. During the captain's absence, Lubitz locked the cockpit door from the inside, preventing anyone from re-entering. He then set the autopilot to descend to 100 feet, initiating a controlled descent that would ultimately lead to the crash.

Over the next ten minutes, air traffic controllers tried to contact the aircraft as it descended, but received no response. The plane steadily lost altitude at a rate of about 3,500 feet per minute. The descent continued uninterrupted, despite repeated attempts by air traffic control and other aircraft to establish contact. Inside the cockpit, Lubitz was breathing normally, indicating he was conscious and in control of the aircraft. The cockpit voice recorder captured the sounds of the captain trying to re-enter the cockpit, banging on the door and shouting, as well as the cries and screams of passengers realizing their impending fate.

At 10:41 AM, the aircraft crashed into the remote area of the French Alps at a speed of approximately 700 km/h (430 mph), instantly killing everyone on board. The crash site was located near

Prads-Haute-Bléone, a rugged and difficult-to-access area, complicating the recovery efforts. Rescue teams faced challenging conditions as they worked to retrieve the remains and the aircraft's black boxes, which were crucial for understanding the events leading up to the crash.

The investigation was led by the French Bureau of Enquiry and Analysis for Civil Aviation Safety (BEA), with assistance from German and Spanish authorities, as well as the FBI. The cockpit voice recorder was recovered shortly after the crash and provided key insights into the final moments of the flight. It revealed Lubitz's deliberate actions and his decision to lock the cockpit door and initiate the fatal descent.

Further investigations uncovered troubling details about Lubitz's mental health history. Lubitz had a history of severe depression and had been deemed unfit to work by several doctors, but this information was not shared with Germanwings or aviation authorities due to strict German privacy laws. He had also sought treatment for vision problems, which he feared might end his career as a pilot. In the days leading up to the crash, Lubitz had researched methods of committing suicide and the security measures of cockpit doors.

The investigation concluded that Lubitz had intentionally crashed the aircraft as an act of suicide, taking the lives of 149 innocent people with him. The findings sparked outrage and grief, leading to intense scrutiny of mental health evaluations and support systems for pilots. The crash raised numerous questions about the balance between patient confidentiality and the need for transparency when public safety is at risk.

In response to the tragedy, aviation authorities worldwide implemented changes to improve cockpit security and pilot mental health assessment. One of the immediate changes was the introduction of the "two-person rule," requiring that at least two authorized personnel be present in the cockpit at all times. This rule aimed to prevent a lone pilot from locking themselves in the cockpit and carrying out similar actions.

Furthermore, airlines and regulatory bodies began reevaluating the mental health screening processes for pilots. There was a push for more rigorous and regular psychological evaluations, as well as the establishment of better support systems for pilots dealing with mental health issues. Lufthansa, the parent company of Germanwings, and other airlines also started implementing measures to encourage pilots to seek help without fear of stigmatization or career repercussions.

The crash of Germanwings Flight 9525 had a profound impact on the aviation industry and highlighted the need for a holistic approach to safety that includes not just technical and procedural measures but also a focus on the mental well-being of flight crew members. It underscored the importance of breaking down the stigma associated with mental health issues and ensuring that those in high-responsibility positions, like pilots, have access to the support and resources they need.

In the years following the crash, the families of the victims advocated for more significant changes and accountability. They called for stricter regulations and better communication between healthcare providers and airlines. The tragedy also prompted a broader societal discussion about mental health, privacy, and safety, influencing policies beyond the aviation industry.

The legacy of Germanwings Flight 9525 is one of sorrow and profound loss, but also of change and reform. The crash serves as a grim reminder of the importance of comprehensive safety measures and the critical need to address mental health issues openly and effectively. It also illustrates the far-reaching consequences that can arise when these factors are neglected or overlooked. The aviation industry continues to learn and evolve from such tragedies, striving to ensure that the skies remain safe for all who travel.

Chapter 12: United Airlines Flight 93

United Airlines Flight 93 was a domestic scheduled passenger flight from Newark International Airport in New Jersey to San Francisco International Airport in California. On September 11, 2001, the Boeing 757-222 operating this flight was hijacked as part of a coordinated terrorist attack orchestrated by the extremist group al-Qaeda. Unlike the other hijacked planes on that day, Flight 93 did not reach its intended target due to the heroic actions of the passengers and crew. Instead, it crashed into a field in Somerset County, Pennsylvania, killing all 44 people on board, including the four hijackers. The story of Flight 93 is one of bravery and sacrifice, standing as a poignant symbol of resistance and courage in the face of terror.

The day began as a typical Tuesday for the 37 passengers and seven crew members on Flight 93. The aircraft was scheduled to depart Newark at 8:00 AM Eastern Time but was delayed until 8:42 AM due to routine traffic congestion. Once airborne, the flight settled into its cross-country route, with the passengers and crew unaware of the unfolding events that would soon change their lives and the world forever.

At approximately 9:28 AM, the hijackers launched their attack. Led by Ziad Jarrah, a trained pilot, and including three other operatives – Ahmed al-Haznawi, Ahmed al-Nami, and Saeed al-Ghamdi – they forcibly entered the cockpit and overpowered the flight crew. The hijackers used box cutters and other makeshift weapons to take control, likely killing or incapacitating Captain Jason Dahl and First Officer LeRoy Homer Jr. in the process. Jarrah assumed control of the aircraft, turning it southeast, toward Washington, D.C., the presumed target being either the White House or the U.S. Capitol.

During the hijacking, the passengers and remaining crew were forced to the back of the plane. Using onboard Airfones and their personal cell phones, several passengers made calls to loved ones, reporting the hijacking and learning about the other attacks that had already occurred that morning – American Airlines Flight 11 and United Airlines Flight 175 had crashed into the World Trade Center towers, and American Airlines Flight 77 had struck the Pentagon. Realizing that their plane was part of a larger terrorist operation, the passengers quickly understood that they were facing a suicide mission.

In a series of extraordinary phone calls, the passengers relayed their situation to the outside world. Todd Beamer, Tom Burnett, Mark Bingham, and Jeremy Glick, among others, spoke to family members and emergency operators. These conversations conveyed the gravity of their situation and the resolve of the passengers to take action. Beamer's famous phrase, "Let's roll," became the rallying cry for their courageous effort to reclaim the aircraft.

The passengers devised a plan to storm the cockpit and overpower the hijackers. Realizing that the hijackers were determined to use the plane as a weapon, the passengers concluded that they had no choice but to fight back, even at the risk of their own lives. Their objective was clear: prevent the hijackers from reaching their intended target and save countless lives on the ground.

At 9:57 AM, the passenger revolt began. They charged down the aisle towards the cockpit, using a food cart to breach the door. The hijackers, realizing they were losing control, violently rocked the plane side to side in a desperate attempt to thwart the attack. The cockpit voice recorder captured the sounds of the struggle, including the passengers' determination and the hijackers' panic.

In the cockpit, Jarrah made drastic maneuvers, including inverting the aircraft and pitching it up and down. Despite these efforts, the passengers continued their assault, undeterred by the chaos. In the final moments, Jarrah, aware that they were about to be overwhelmed, deliberately crashed the plane into a field near Shanksville, Pennsylvania, at 10:03 AM. The impact obliterated the aircraft, killing everyone on board instantly.

The crash site quickly became a scene of intense investigation and solemn remembrance. The debris field was scattered over a wide area, but the efforts of recovery teams ensured that crucial evidence was collected, including the flight data recorder and cockpit voice recorder. These recordings provided invaluable insights into the final minutes of Flight 93, documenting the passengers' heroic attempt to thwart the hijackers.

The actions of the passengers and crew of United Airlines Flight 93 are credited with preventing a catastrophic attack on the nation's capital. Their bravery and selflessness likely saved countless lives and averted further destruction on that fateful day. The passengers' decision to fight back was a profound act of courage that resonated deeply with the American public and the world.

In the aftermath of the attacks, Flight 93 became a symbol of heroism and national resilience. The field where the plane crashed was designated as a national memorial. The Flight 93 National Memorial, established by an Act of Congress in 2002, honors the passengers and crew members who fought back against their hijackers. The memorial, dedicated in 2011, features a visitor center, a wall of names, and the Tower of Voices, which holds 40 wind chimes representing each person who lost their life.

The legacy of Flight 93 also influenced national security policies. The events of September 11, 2001, led to significant changes in aviation security, including the reinforcement of cockpit doors, enhanced screening procedures, and the creation of the Transportation Security Administration (TSA). The collective trauma of the attacks underscored the need for vigilance and preparedness against terrorism.

In the years following the tragedy, the families of the victims of Flight 93 have worked to preserve their loved ones' memory and advocate for lasting change. They have shared their stories, participated in the development of the memorial, and engaged in public speaking to honor the legacy of the passengers and crew. Their efforts ensure that the bravery and sacrifice of those on Flight 93 are never forgotten.

The story of United Airlines Flight 93 is a poignant reminder of the resilience of the human spirit in the face of unimaginable adversity. It illustrates the capacity for ordinary people to perform extraordinary acts of courage and selflessness. The passengers and crew of Flight 93 showed that even in the darkest moments, the strength and resolve of individuals can shine through, leaving a legacy of hope and heroism that continues to inspire.

Chapter 13: Japan Airlines Flight 123

Japan Airlines Flight 123 is one of the most tragic and significant aviation disasters in history. The flight, a domestic service from Tokyo's Haneda Airport to Osaka International Airport, met with a catastrophic failure on August 12, 1985, leading to the deadliest single-aircraft accident in aviation history. The Boeing 747SR-46, registration JA8119, crashed into Mount Takamagahara in Ueno, Gunma Prefecture, Japan, resulting in the deaths of 520 of the 524 occupants. This disaster not only highlighted severe lapses in aircraft maintenance but also underscored the importance of safety protocols and emergency response mechanisms.

Flight 123 was a regular evening flight scheduled to depart Haneda at 6:00 PM and arrive in Osaka about an hour later. The Boeing 747SR, a short-range variant of the 747, was carrying 509 passengers and 15 crew members. Among the passengers were many families returning from summer holidays, making the crash especially heartbreaking due to the number of children on board.

The aircraft departed Haneda at 6:12 PM, slightly behind schedule. The takeoff and initial climb were uneventful. However, approximately 12 minutes after takeoff, at around 6:24 PM, a loud noise was heard, followed by rapid decompression. The rear pressure bulkhead had failed, causing explosive decompression that blew off a large portion of the vertical stabilizer and severed all four hydraulic lines. This catastrophic failure severely compromised the aircraft's control systems.

The root cause of the bulkhead failure traced back to improper repairs conducted seven years earlier. In 1978, the aircraft had suffered a tailstrike, damaging the rear pressure bulkhead. The repair work, performed by Boeing, was found to be flawed. The damaged bulkhead had been repaired using a doubler plate that did not conform to Boeing's repair procedures. Instead of a single continuous doubler plate, two separate plates were used, creating a critical weakness. Over the years, this improper repair led to fatigue cracks that gradually expanded until the bulkhead failed catastrophically.

With the loss of the vertical stabilizer and the severance of all four hydraulic systems, the crew faced a dire situation. The aircraft became nearly uncontrollable, yawing and pitching wildly. Despite the catastrophic damage, the pilots, led by Captain Masami Takahama, First Officer Yutaka Sasaki, Flight Engineer Hiroshi Fukuda, and Flight Engineer-in-training Hideyuki Nagahama, displayed remarkable skill and determination in attempting to control the crippled aircraft.

For the next 32 minutes, the crew battled to keep the aircraft aloft, using engine thrust differentials to steer and control altitude. The cockpit voice recorder (CVR) captured the intense and desperate struggle as the pilots communicated with air traffic control and each other, trying to stabilize the plane. The crew's valiant efforts enabled the aircraft to remain in the air, giving a brief glimmer of hope that they might manage an emergency landing.

At around 6:56 PM, the crew attempted to make an emergency landing at Haneda Airport. However, their efforts were thwarted by the lack of effective control. The aircraft continued to oscillate uncontrollably, and at 6:58 PM, it struck Mount Takamagahara at an altitude of 1,565 meters (5,135 feet). The impact resulted in a devastating crash, breaking the aircraft into multiple pieces and scattering debris over a wide area.

Despite the remote location of the crash site, the impact was witnessed by locals, who immediately reported the incident. Rescue operations were delayed due to the difficult terrain and the time it took for search and rescue teams to locate the wreckage. The first ground rescue teams did not reach the site until the following morning. Tragically, this delay likely cost lives, as several passengers initially survived the crash but succumbed to their injuries before help arrived.

Among the survivors was a 12-year-old girl named Keiko Kawakami, found trapped in the wreckage along with three other passengers: Hirokazu Kurakami, a 34-year-old auto sales manager; Yumi Ochiai, a 25-year-old off-duty flight attendant; and 8-year-old Mikiko Yoshizaki. Their survival stories, particularly the resilience shown by young Keiko, brought a glimmer of solace amid the overwhelming grief.

The aftermath of the crash led to a comprehensive investigation by the Japan Transport Ministry and other aviation authorities. The investigation revealed the flawed repair on the rear pressure bulkhead as the primary cause. Boeing's maintenance procedures had been improperly followed, and the repair's inherent weakness had gone undetected for years, ultimately leading to the catastrophic failure.

The investigation's findings prompted significant changes in aircraft maintenance and safety protocols. Boeing reviewed and revised its maintenance and repair procedures to ensure strict adherence to safety standards. The airline industry globally re-evaluated safety protocols, emphasizing the importance of rigorous maintenance and thorough inspections, particularly for repairs on critical structural components.

In response to the disaster, Japan Airlines also implemented substantial changes to its safety and maintenance operations. The airline established a dedicated safety promotion center and increased its focus on maintenance quality assurance. The crash also led to changes in how airlines and manufacturers handle accident investigations and communication, fostering a culture of transparency and continuous improvement in aviation safety.

The legacy of Japan Airlines Flight 123 extends beyond the immediate technical and procedural changes. The tragedy deeply affected the families of the victims and the broader Japanese society. Memorial services and monuments have been erected to honor the memory of those who perished. The incident serves as a solemn reminder of the critical importance of safety in aviation and the devastating consequences of lapses in maintenance and oversight.

For the families of the victims, the crash left an indelible mark, a source of profound grief and loss. Over the years, survivors and relatives have sought to keep the memory of their loved ones alive, advocating for continued vigilance in aviation safety to prevent such a disaster from ever happening again. Annual memorial services are held at the crash site, where families, aviation professionals, and members of the public gather to pay their respects and reflect on the lessons learned from the tragedy.

The crash of Japan Airlines Flight 123 remains a pivotal event in aviation history, illustrating the complex interplay of engineering, maintenance, and human factors that contribute to air safety. The lessons drawn from this disaster continue to shape the aviation industry's approach to safety, ensuring that the sacrifices of those who perished are not forgotten, and that their legacy contributes to the ongoing pursuit of safer skies for all.

Chapter 14: Tenerife Airport Disaster

The Tenerife Airport Disaster remains the deadliest aviation accident in history. On March 27, 1977, two Boeing 747 jumbo jets collided on the runway of Los Rodeos Airport (now Tenerife North Airport) in the Canary Islands, Spain. The disaster resulted in the deaths of 583 people out of the 644 aboard the two aircraft. This catastrophe was the outcome of a series of unfortunate events, miscommunications, and errors, highlighting the critical importance of clear communication and effective air traffic control in aviation safety.

The disaster involved two flights: KLM Royal Dutch Airlines Flight 4805 and Pan American World Airways (Pan Am) Flight 1736. Both aircraft were scheduled to fly from their respective origins to Gran Canaria Airport in Las Palmas, the Canary Islands' primary airport. However, a terrorist bombing incident at Gran Canaria forced the temporary closure of the airport, diverting numerous incoming flights to Los Rodeos Airport on the nearby island of Tenerife.

KLM Flight 4805, a charter flight from Amsterdam, carried 248 passengers and crew, while Pan Am Flight 1736, a scheduled flight from Los Angeles to New York with a stopover in Tenerife, carried 396 passengers and crew. Upon arrival at Los Rodeos, both flights were instructed to park on the airport's main taxiway due to the limited parking space at the small airport, which was not equipped to handle such a high volume of large aircraft.

The airport soon became congested, with several other diverted aircraft occupying the limited apron and taxiway space. The weather conditions, initially clear, began to deteriorate as the day progressed, with heavy fog rolling in, reducing visibility significantly. This added another layer of complexity to an already challenging situation.

Around 4:00 PM, the Gran Canaria Airport reopened, and the aircraft at Los Rodeos prepared for departure. Pan Am 1736 was instructed to taxi down the main runway and then exit via a taxiway to reach the parallel taxiway. However, due to the fog, the crew missed the designated taxiway and continued down the runway. Meanwhile, KLM 4805, which had been refueled and was ready for departure, was instructed to taxi into position at the end of the same runway and hold until receiving clearance for takeoff.

Here, a critical series of miscommunications and misunderstandings unfolded. The KLM aircraft, piloted by Captain Jacob Veldhuyzen van Zanten, an experienced and respected training captain for KLM, misunderstood the instructions from the tower. Believing they had received clearance for takeoff, Captain Van Zanten initiated the takeoff roll. The Pan Am crew, realizing the KLM aircraft was accelerating towards them on the same runway, desperately attempted to communicate the danger to the control tower.

The dense fog severely hampered visibility for both the air traffic controllers and the flight crews. As the KLM aircraft sped down the runway, the Pan Am crew frantically tried to maneuver their aircraft off the runway. However, the massive Boeing 747 could not clear the path in time. At 5:06 PM, the KLM aircraft, traveling at high speed, collided with the Pan Am plane. The impact was catastrophic.

The KLM aircraft's nose gear lifted off the ground, but its fuselage struck the upper fuselage of the Pan Am aircraft, ripping it apart. The collision ignited the full fuel tanks of the KLM 747, creating a massive fireball. The force of the impact and subsequent explosion resulted in the immediate deaths of most occupants on both aircraft. Miraculously, there were some survivors, primarily in the front section of the Pan Am aircraft, but the majority of the passengers and crew on both planes perished.

The investigation into the disaster was led by Spanish authorities, with the cooperation of Dutch, American, and other international aviation experts. The analysis of the cockpit voice recorders (CVRs) and flight data recorders (FDRs), combined with testimonies from the survivors and air traffic controllers, revealed several key factors that contributed to the tragedy.

Firstly, the investigation highlighted the critical role of miscommunication and language barriers. The KLM captain had misunderstood the tower's clearance instructions, interpreting the message as clearance for immediate takeoff. The lack of standardized phraseology and the non-native English language proficiency of the KLM crew contributed to the misinterpretation.

Secondly, the investigation pointed out the deficiencies in the airport's infrastructure. Los Rodeos Airport was not equipped to handle the sudden influx of large aircraft diverted from Gran Canaria. The limited taxiway space forced aircraft to taxi on the runway, creating a hazardous situation, especially under low-visibility conditions.

Thirdly, human factors played a significant role. Captain Van Zanten's reputation and authority as KLM's chief training captain may have contributed to a cockpit environment where his actions were not adequately questioned by the co-pilot and flight engineer. The concept of cockpit resource management (CRM), which emphasizes effective communication and teamwork among flight crew members, was still in its infancy at the time. The hierarchical nature of cockpit dynamics likely prevented the junior crew members from challenging the captain's premature takeoff decision.

The disaster led to significant changes in aviation safety protocols and practices. The International Civil Aviation Organization (ICAO) and national aviation authorities worldwide adopted more stringent communication protocols to prevent misunderstandings. Standardized phraseology for air traffic control clearances became mandatory, reducing the risk of misinterpretation.

The tragedy also underscored the importance of CRM training, which became a standard part of flight crew training programs globally. CRM focuses on fostering open communication, teamwork, and decision-making among flight crews, ensuring that all crew members can voice concerns and challenge decisions if safety is at risk.

The physical infrastructure of airports also saw improvements. Airports worldwide, particularly those in regions prone to fog or adverse weather conditions, enhanced their ground radar systems and runway lighting to improve visibility and safety during low-visibility operations. The disaster also spurred advancements in runway incursion prevention technologies.

In the aftermath, the families of the victims sought solace and justice. Memorials were erected in honor of the victims, including a monument at the crash site in Tenerife. The aviation industry learned invaluable lessons from the tragedy, ensuring that the mistakes and miscommunications that led to the disaster would not be repeated.

The Tenerife Airport Disaster remains a stark reminder of the complexities and dangers inherent in aviation. The convergence of miscommunication, human error, and inadequate infrastructure created a perfect storm that resulted in unimaginable loss. However, the lessons learned from the tragedy have driven substantial improvements in aviation safety, benefiting future generations of travelers. The legacy of the disaster is a testament to the continuous efforts to enhance the safety and reliability of air travel, ensuring that such a calamity never occurs again.

Chapter 15: American Airlines Flight 191

American Airlines Flight 191, a McDonnell Douglas DC-10-10, was scheduled to fly from Chicago O'Hare International Airport to Los Angeles International Airport on May 25, 1979. Tragically, this flight ended in one of the deadliest aviation accidents in U.S. history, resulting in the deaths of all 271 people on board and two people on the ground. The disaster had far-reaching consequences for aviation safety and the design and maintenance of the DC-10 aircraft.

Flight 191 was operated by a three-engine McDonnell Douglas DC-10, a popular wide-body jet used extensively by airlines for long-haul flights. The aircraft involved in the accident was tail number N110AA, delivered to American Airlines in February 1972. On that fateful day, the flight was scheduled to depart from Chicago at 2:45 PM CDT.

The aircraft was piloted by Captain Walter Lux, First Officer James Dillard, and Flight Engineer Alfred Udovich. Captain Lux was an experienced pilot with more than 22,000 flight hours, including over 3,000 hours on the DC-10. First Officer Dillard had logged over 9,000 flight hours, with about 1,000 hours on the DC-10, while Flight Engineer Udovich had over 15,000 flight hours, including 1,800 hours on the DC-10.

The flight began normally, with the aircraft taxiing to Runway 32R for takeoff. The weather was clear, and the runway was dry. At 2:59 PM, Flight 191 was cleared for takeoff. The aircraft began its takeoff roll, accelerating down the runway. However, just as the plane was lifting off the ground, a catastrophic event occurred.

At approximately 6,000 feet down the runway and at an altitude of about 300 feet, the aircraft's left engine (Engine No. 1) suddenly separated from the wing. The engine, along with its pylon, flipped over the top of the wing and landed on the runway. This violent separation caused significant damage to the wing structure, including the hydraulic systems that controlled the leading-edge slats on the left wing.

The loss of the engine and the damage to the wing had immediate and severe consequences. The leading-edge slats on the left wing, which are crucial for maintaining lift at low speeds, retracted due to the hydraulic failure. This caused the left wing to lose lift, resulting in an aerodynamic stall. The aircraft rolled to the left and began to lose altitude rapidly.

Despite the dire situation, the flight crew attempted to control the aircraft. They followed emergency procedures, reducing thrust on the remaining engines to counteract the roll. However, the damage was too severe, and the aircraft continued to roll leftward. Within seconds, the DC-10 was in an unrecoverable position, banked sharply to the left.

At 3:03 PM, less than a minute after takeoff, Flight 191 crashed into an open field near a trailer park located about a mile from the end of the runway. The impact caused a massive explosion, creating a large fireball that was visible for miles. The crash destroyed numerous trailers and vehicles in the trailer park, causing additional fatalities on the ground.

The immediate aftermath was chaotic, with emergency responders rushing to the scene. Despite their rapid response, the intensity of the fire and the devastation at the crash site made rescue efforts difficult. The fire was so intense that it took several hours to extinguish completely. The crash site was a scene of utter destruction, with wreckage scattered over a wide area.

The National Transportation Safety Board (NTSB) launched a comprehensive investigation into the accident. The investigation team faced numerous challenges, including the extensive damage to the aircraft and the need to recover and analyze the various components scattered across the crash site. The primary focus was on determining the cause of the engine separation and the subsequent loss of control.

The investigation revealed several critical findings. The immediate cause of the engine separation was traced to a maintenance procedure that had been performed eight weeks before the accident. During this procedure, the engine and pylon assembly had been removed and reinstalled for routine maintenance. However, the method used by American Airlines maintenance personnel deviated from the manufacturer's recommended procedure.

Instead of removing the engine and pylon separately, the maintenance crew had opted to remove them as a single unit. This practice, although intended to save time, introduced significant stress on the pylon's attachment points during reinstallation. This stress led to the development of a fatigue crack in the pylon's aft bulkhead, which eventually caused the catastrophic failure on Flight 191.

The NTSB also identified deficiencies in the oversight and communication between McDonnell Douglas and the airlines operating the DC-10. The manufacturer was aware that some airlines were using alternative maintenance procedures but did not issue clear guidance or warnings about the potential risks. This lack of communication and oversight contributed to the conditions that led to the accident.

Another critical factor in the crash was the design of the DC-10's hydraulic system. The separation of the engine and the subsequent damage to the wing resulted in the loss of hydraulic pressure needed to keep the leading-edge slats deployed. This design vulnerability meant that a single point of failure could have catastrophic consequences for the aircraft's controllability.

The investigation also highlighted the need for improved training and emergency procedures for flight crews. While the flight crew of Flight 191 acted in accordance with their training, the rapid sequence of events and the severity of the damage left them with little chance of regaining control. The NTSB recommended enhancements to pilot training programs to better prepare crews for similar emergencies.

In response to the findings of the investigation, several significant changes were implemented in the aviation industry. The Federal Aviation Administration (FAA) mandated revisions to the maintenance procedures for the DC-10 and other similar aircraft, ensuring that manufacturers' guidelines were strictly followed. The FAA also required modifications to the design of the DC-10's hydraulic and flight control systems to enhance their redundancy and reliability.

American Airlines, along with other carriers operating the DC-10, reviewed and revised their maintenance practices to prevent similar incidents. The airline industry as a whole adopted more stringent oversight and communication protocols between manufacturers, maintenance personnel, and regulatory authorities. These changes were aimed at improving safety and preventing maintenance-related failures.

The accident also had a profound impact on the development of future aircraft designs. The vulnerabilities exposed by the crash of Flight 191 influenced the design philosophy of subsequent aircraft models, emphasizing redundancy, fail-safe mechanisms, and robust maintenance procedures. The lessons learned from the disaster contributed to the evolution of safer and more reliable commercial airliners.

The legacy of Flight 191 is marked by the profound loss of life and the significant changes it brought to aviation safety. Memorials were established to honor the victims, including a permanent memorial at the crash site in Des Plaines, Illinois. The tragedy served as a somber reminder of the critical importance of adherence to maintenance procedures, effective communication, and rigorous oversight in ensuring the safety of air travel.

The disaster of American Airlines Flight 191 remains a pivotal moment in aviation history. It underscores the need for constant vigilance, continuous improvement, and a relentless commitment to safety in the aviation industry. The changes implemented in the aftermath of the accident have contributed to making air travel one of the safest modes of transportation today, honoring the memory of those who lost their lives on that fateful day in 1979.

Chapter 16: Swissair Flight 111

Swissair Flight 111 was a scheduled international passenger flight from New York City's John F. Kennedy International Airport (JFK) to Geneva, Switzerland. On September 2, 1998, the McDonnell Douglas MD-11 aircraft operating the flight crashed into the Atlantic Ocean near Peggy's Cove, Nova Scotia, Canada, killing all 229 passengers and crew aboard. The crash of Swissair Flight 111 is one of the deadliest aviation disasters involving an MD-11 and led to significant changes in aviation safety regulations, particularly regarding in-flight fire prevention and cabin materials.

The aircraft involved in the disaster was a McDonnell Douglas MD-11, registered as HB-IWF. It had been delivered to Swissair in 1991 and had accumulated approximately 36,000 flight hours over the course of 5,800 flights. The MD-11 was a wide-body airliner with three engines, designed as an improvement over the earlier DC-10. Swissair, known for its high safety standards and excellent service, operated the aircraft with a configuration that included first-class, business-class, and economy-class seating.

On the evening of September 2, 1998, Swissair Flight 111 departed from JFK Airport at 8:18 PM Eastern Daylight Time (EDT) with 215 passengers and 14 crew members on board. The flight was under the command of Captain Urs Zimmermann, a highly experienced pilot with over 10,800 flight hours, and First Officer Stefan Löw, who had over 4,800 flight hours. Both pilots were well-regarded for their professionalism and expertise.

The initial part of the flight proceeded normally. The aircraft climbed to its cruising altitude of 33,000 feet and followed its planned route northeastward over the Atlantic Ocean, heading towards the Canadian Maritimes. The weather conditions were favorable, and the flight crew maintained routine communication with air traffic control.

Approximately 53 minutes after takeoff, at around 9:11 PM, the flight crew detected an unusual odor in the cockpit, followed by visible smoke. The captain and first officer began troubleshooting to identify the source of the smoke. They initially suspected an air conditioning or avionics problem and began following the checklist procedures for smoke removal.

The situation quickly deteriorated as the smoke intensified, prompting the crew to declare an emergency at 9:14 PM and request an immediate diversion to the nearest airport. Air traffic control directed the flight to Halifax International Airport (now Halifax Stanfield International Airport), located about 66 nautical miles away. The crew began descending from their cruising altitude in preparation for an emergency landing.

As the aircraft descended through 21,000 feet, the situation in the cockpit worsened. The smoke thickened, and critical systems began to fail. The flight data recorder (FDR) and cockpit voice recorder (CVR) captured the increasing urgency and difficulty faced by the pilots as they struggled to maintain control of the aircraft and manage the emergency.

At 9:24 PM, the flight crew informed air traffic control that they needed to dump fuel to reduce the aircraft's weight for landing. They were directed to a holding pattern over St. Margaret's Bay, near Peggy's Cove, to perform the fuel dump. The crew initiated the fuel dumping procedure and continued to communicate with air traffic control about their intentions and actions.

However, as the fuel dump proceeded, the situation on board deteriorated rapidly. The fire, which had initially been confined to the area above the cockpit ceiling, spread to the aircraft's wiring and other critical systems. The loss of electrical power and the incapacitating effects of smoke and fire overwhelmed the crew's ability to control the aircraft. Communication with air traffic control became sporadic and increasingly frantic.

At 10:31 PM, the flight data recorder stopped recording, indicating a complete electrical failure. Moments later, at 10:31:18 PM, the aircraft crashed into the Atlantic Ocean approximately 5 nautical miles southwest of Peggy's Cove. The impact was catastrophic, and the aircraft disintegrated upon hitting the water, scattering debris over a wide area.

The search and recovery operation began immediately. Canadian and international search and rescue teams, including military and civilian resources, were mobilized to locate and recover the wreckage and victims. The Royal Canadian Mounted Police (RCMP) and Canadian Coast Guard played crucial roles in the operation, which was hampered by rough seas and challenging weather conditions.

Despite these difficulties, recovery teams were able to locate the main wreckage site and recover significant portions of the aircraft, including the flight data recorder and cockpit voice recorder. The search and recovery efforts continued for several weeks, eventually leading to the recovery of all 229 victims.

The investigation into the crash of Swissair Flight 111 was conducted by the Transportation Safety Board of Canada (TSB) with the assistance of international aviation experts, including representatives from the National Transportation Safety Board (NTSB) of the United States and other relevant agencies. The investigation was one of the most complex and thorough in aviation history, lasting over four years and resulting in a final report published in March 2003.

The investigation determined that the fire originated in the cockpit area, likely caused by an electrical fault that ignited flammable materials in the aircraft's insulation. The insulation material, a metalized polyethylene terephthalate (MPET), was highly flammable and contributed to the rapid spread of the fire. The fire's progression led to the failure of critical systems, including the aircraft's electrical and avionics systems, ultimately rendering the aircraft uncontrollable.

The TSB's final report identified several key factors that contributed to the disaster:

1. **Flammable Materials**: The use of MPET insulation, which was highly flammable and not adequately tested for fire resistance, played a significant role in the rapid spread of the fire.

2. **Electrical Faults**: The initial ignition source was traced to an electrical fault, possibly involving the in-flight entertainment system's wiring, which was not installed according to approved specifications.

3. **Inadequate Fire Detection and Suppression**: The aircraft's fire detection and suppression systems were not capable of effectively detecting and combating a fire in the hidden areas above the cockpit ceiling.

4. **Crew Procedures**: The emergency procedures and checklists available to the flight crew did not adequately address the severity of the in-flight fire, delaying their ability to take decisive action.

In response to the findings, the TSB issued several safety recommendations to improve aviation safety and prevent similar disasters in the future. These recommendations included:

1. **Improved Fire Safety Standards**: The introduction of more stringent standards for materials used in aircraft construction, particularly those related to fire resistance and toxicity.

2. **Enhanced Fire Detection and Suppression**: The development and installation of advanced fire detection and suppression systems capable of addressing fires in hidden areas of the aircraft.

3. **Revised Crew Training and Procedures**: Enhancements to crew training programs and emergency procedures to better

equip flight crews to handle in-flight fires and other emergencies.

4. **Electrical System Modifications**: Improvements to the design and installation of electrical systems to reduce the risk of electrical faults and fires.

The crash of Swissair Flight 111 also had a profound impact on the airline industry and regulatory agencies worldwide. The International Civil Aviation Organization (ICAO) and other aviation authorities adopted many of the TSB's recommendations, leading to widespread changes in aircraft design, maintenance practices, and safety protocols.

For the families and loved ones of the victims, the tragedy of Swissair Flight 111 was a devastating loss. Memorials were established to honor the memory of those who perished, including a permanent memorial site near Peggy's Cove. The disaster remains a somber reminder of the critical importance of safety in aviation and the need for continuous improvement to protect passengers and crew.

The legacy of Swissair Flight 111 endures through the significant changes it spurred in aviation safety. The lessons learned from the investigation have contributed to making air travel safer, ensuring that the sacrifices of those who lost their lives were not in vain. The ongoing commitment to enhancing safety standards and procedures in the aviation industry is a testament to the enduring impact of this tragic event.

Chapter 17: EgyptAir Flight 990

EgyptAir Flight 990 was a regularly scheduled international passenger flight from Los Angeles International Airport (LAX) to Cairo International Airport, with a stopover at John F. Kennedy International Airport (JFK) in New York City. On October 31, 1999, the Boeing 767-366ER aircraft operating the flight crashed into the Atlantic Ocean approximately 60 miles south of Nantucket Island, Massachusetts. All 217 people on board perished. The crash of EgyptAir Flight 990 remains one of the most controversial and tragic events in aviation history due to the unresolved debate over the causes of the crash, which pitted the U.S. National Transportation Safety Board (NTSB) against the Egyptian Civil Aviation Authority (ECAA).

The aircraft involved in the accident was a Boeing 767-366ER, registration SU-GAP, and it had been delivered to EgyptAir in September 1989. The aircraft had accumulated over 33,000 flight hours and 7,400 flight cycles. It was equipped with two Pratt & Whitney PW4000 engines and had a seating configuration that included first-class, business-class, and economy-class sections.

On October 31, 1999, EgyptAir Flight 990 departed from Los Angeles at 1:20 AM PST. After a routine flight to JFK, the aircraft landed and underwent a crew change before departing for Cairo. The flight crew for the JFK to Cairo leg consisted of Captain Ahmed El-Habashi, First Officer Adel Anwar, relief Captain Raouf Noureldin, and relief First Officer Gameel Al-Batouti. There were also 14 flight attendants on board, along with 203 passengers, many of whom were American tourists returning from vacations in Egypt, Egyptian nationals, and several other international travelers.

The aircraft departed JFK at 1:19 AM EST on October 31, 1999. The initial phase of the flight proceeded normally, with the aircraft climbing to its cruising altitude of 33,000 feet. The flight plan called for a routine route across the Atlantic, with the estimated flight time to Cairo being around 10 hours.

At approximately 1:50 AM, while the aircraft was cruising at 33,000 feet, the cockpit voice recorder (CVR) captured Captain El-Habashi announcing that he was leaving the cockpit for a short break, leaving First Officer Batouti in command. Shortly after the captain left, the CVR recorded First Officer Batouti uttering a phrase in Arabic, "Tawkalt ala Allah," which translates to "I rely on God."

Moments later, the aircraft began a rapid and uncommanded descent. The flight data recorder (FDR) showed that the aircraft's autopilot was disengaged, and the nose pitched down sharply. The Boeing 767 descended at an alarming rate, dropping 14,000 feet in just 36 seconds. The FDR also indicated that both engines were cut off and the elevator control inputs were pushing the nose of the aircraft further down.

As the aircraft descended through 19,000 feet, Captain El-Habashi returned to the cockpit and exclaimed, "What's happening? What's happening?" Despite his attempts to regain control, the aircraft continued its descent. At around 16,000 feet, the FDR recorded a brief recovery attempt where the nose pitched up momentarily. However, the downward plunge resumed, and the aircraft eventually entered a near-vertical dive.

At 2:00 AM, after plummeting for nearly two minutes, EgyptAir Flight 990 impacted the Atlantic Ocean at a speed exceeding 400 knots. The force of the impact disintegrated the aircraft, and all 217 occupants were killed instantly. The wreckage was scattered over a wide area on the ocean floor, complicating recovery efforts.

The U.S. Coast Guard, Navy, and numerous other agencies were immediately mobilized to search for survivors and recover the wreckage. Despite the challenging conditions, search and recovery operations were conducted, and significant portions of the aircraft, including the flight recorders, were eventually recovered from the ocean floor. The NTSB was tasked with leading the investigation, with the ECAA providing assistance.

The investigation into the crash of EgyptAir Flight 990 was complex and contentious from the outset. The NTSB's primary focus was to determine the cause of the rapid descent and subsequent crash. The analysis of the flight recorders and wreckage provided crucial insights into the sequence of events, but also raised numerous questions.

The NTSB's investigation revealed that the uncommanded descent was initiated by actions taken by First Officer Batouti, who was alone in the cockpit at the time. The evidence indicated that Batouti had disengaged the autopilot, cut off both engines, and pushed the control yoke forward to initiate the dive. The recorded phrase, "I rely on God," and Batouti's control inputs were central to the NTSB's findings.

The NTSB concluded that the crash was a result of deliberate actions by First Officer Batouti. The board's final report, published in March 2002, determined that the probable cause of the accident was the intentional manipulation of the flight controls by Batouti. This conclusion was based on the absence of any mechanical failure or external factors that could have caused the descent. The report also noted that there was no indication of a struggle or incapacitation of Batouti, further supporting the theory of deliberate action.

However, the Egyptian Civil Aviation Authority (ECAA) strongly disagreed with the NTSB's findings. The ECAA argued that the crash was the result of a mechanical failure, possibly involving the aircraft's elevator control system. They suggested that Batouti's actions were a response to a malfunction, rather than the cause of the crash. The ECAA's position was that Batouti was attempting to troubleshoot and recover the aircraft when the accident occurred.

The differing conclusions between the NTSB and the ECAA led to a highly contentious and politically charged debate. The ECAA's assertion of a mechanical failure was supported by some independent experts and analysts, who pointed to the possibility of a rudder or elevator control issue. However, the NTSB's extensive investigation found no evidence of such a failure, and the board maintained that the actions of First Officer Batouti were intentional.

The controversy surrounding the crash of EgyptAir Flight 990 had significant implications for aviation safety and international cooperation in accident investigations. The incident highlighted the challenges of cross-cultural and inter-agency collaboration in determining the causes of aviation accidents. It also underscored the importance of thorough and unbiased investigations to ensure the accuracy and credibility of findings.

In the wake of the crash, several safety measures and procedural changes were implemented to enhance aviation safety. These included:

1. **Enhanced Security Protocols**: Airlines and aviation authorities introduced stricter security protocols for flight crew members, including psychological screening and monitoring, to identify and address potential risks.

2. **Improved Cockpit Procedures**: Changes were made to cockpit procedures to ensure that two qualified pilots were present in the cockpit at all times during critical phases of flight. This measure aimed to prevent situations where one pilot could act alone without oversight.

3. **Increased Focus on Mental Health**: The aviation industry placed greater emphasis on the mental health and well-being of flight crews. Programs were developed to provide support and resources for pilots dealing with stress, depression, or other psychological issues.

4. **Advanced Flight Data Monitoring**: Airlines implemented advanced flight data monitoring systems to track and analyze flight crew actions and aircraft performance in real time. This technology allowed for early detection of unusual or

potentially unsafe behavior.

5. **Enhanced Training Programs**: Pilot training programs were revised to include more comprehensive emergency and abnormal situation training. This training ensured that pilots were better prepared to handle unexpected events and mechanical failures.

Despite these improvements, the crash of EgyptAir Flight 990 remains a deeply tragic and unresolved event. The loss of 217 lives was a devastating blow to the families and loved ones of the victims, as well as to the aviation community. Memorials were established to honor the victims, including a permanent memorial at the crash site off the coast of Nantucket.

The legacy of EgyptAir Flight 990 is marked by the ongoing quest for truth and the continuous efforts to improve aviation safety. The controversy and debate surrounding the crash serve as a reminder of the complexities and challenges involved in aviation accident investigations. The lessons learned from this tragedy have contributed to making air travel safer, ensuring that the sacrifices of those who

Chapter 18: SilkAir Flight 185

SilkAir Flight 185 was a scheduled international passenger flight from Jakarta, Indonesia, to Singapore, operated by a Boeing 737-36N. On December 19, 1997, the aircraft crashed into the Musi River near Palembang, Indonesia, killing all 104 passengers and crew on board. The crash of SilkAir Flight 185 is one of the most controversial and debated aviation disasters in history, primarily due to conflicting conclusions regarding the cause of the crash reached by Indonesian and American investigators.

The aircraft involved in the accident was a Boeing 737-36N, registered as 9V-TRF. It was relatively new, having been delivered to SilkAir in February 1997, and had accumulated approximately 2,238 flight hours over the course of 1,307 flight cycles. The Boeing 737-300 series is a short- to medium-range narrow-body jet, known for its reliability and efficiency. SilkAir, a regional subsidiary of Singapore Airlines, had a reputation for maintaining high standards of safety and service.

On December 19, 1997, SilkAir Flight 185 departed from Jakarta's Soekarno-Hatta International Airport at 3:37 PM local time, bound for Singapore Changi Airport. The flight was commanded by Captain Tsu Way Ming, a highly experienced pilot with over 7,173 flight hours, including 2,238 hours on the Boeing 737. First Officer Duncan Ward, a New Zealander with 2,501 flight hours, including 1,032 hours on the Boeing 737, served as the co-pilot. There were five flight attendants on board and 97 passengers from various countries, including Indonesia, Singapore, and several other nations.

The initial part of the flight proceeded normally. The aircraft climbed to its cruising altitude of 35,000 feet and followed its planned route over the Java Sea. The weather conditions were reported as good, with clear skies and no significant turbulence. Communication between the flight crew and air traffic control was routine and uneventful.

At approximately 4:05 PM, around 23 minutes after takeoff, the cockpit voice recorder (CVR) and flight data recorder (FDR) suddenly stopped recording. The loss of both recorders simultaneously was highly unusual and indicated a significant disruption to the aircraft's power systems. Despite this, the aircraft continued to transmit radar signals, allowing air traffic controllers to track its position and altitude.

Shortly after the recorders ceased functioning, the aircraft began an unexpected and rapid descent. Radar data showed that the Boeing 737 entered a steep dive from its cruising altitude of 35,000 feet. The descent rate was extremely high, reaching speeds in excess of the aircraft's design limits. Within a matter of minutes, SilkAir Flight 185 crashed into the Musi River at high speed, disintegrating upon impact. The force of the crash was so severe that it caused the aircraft to break apart, scattering debris over a wide area and making recovery efforts extremely challenging.

Search and recovery operations commenced immediately, involving Indonesian authorities, military personnel, and international experts. The remote location of the crash site and the difficult terrain added to the complexity of the recovery efforts. Divers and search teams worked tirelessly to retrieve wreckage and locate the remains of the victims. Over the following weeks, significant portions of the aircraft were recovered, including the engines, landing gear, and various other components. However, the impact forces and underwater environment had severely damaged many parts of the aircraft, complicating the investigation.

The investigation into the crash of SilkAir Flight 185 was led by Indonesia's National Transportation Safety Committee (NTSC), with assistance from the U.S. National Transportation Safety Board (NTSB), the Federal Aviation Administration (FAA), and Boeing. The primary focus of the investigation was to determine the cause of the sudden descent and the loss of control that led to the crash.

The analysis of the wreckage and available data revealed several critical findings. The primary concern was the simultaneous loss of the CVR and FDR, which suggested a severe electrical or structural failure. However, investigators were unable to identify any specific mechanical failure or malfunction that could have caused the recorders to stop working. The recovered wreckage showed no evidence of in-flight fire, explosion, or catastrophic structural failure prior to impact.

One of the most contentious aspects of the investigation was the examination of the flight crew's actions and possible involvement in the crash. The NTSC and the NTSB conducted extensive reviews of the pilots' backgrounds, psychological profiles, and personal circumstances. Captain Tsu was a well-respected and experienced pilot with no history of disciplinary issues or concerns about his professional conduct. However, some reports suggested that he had experienced personal and financial difficulties in the months leading up to the crash.

The NTSB's investigation concluded that the most likely cause of the crash was intentional action by one of the pilots. The NTSB's analysis was based on the flight profile during the final moments, which showed a controlled dive consistent with deliberate input on the flight controls. The absence of mechanical anomalies and the sudden cessation of the flight recorders further supported the theory of pilot involvement. The NTSB's final report, published in December 2000, stated that the crash was likely the result of "intentional actions by a crewmember," although it did not specifically identify which pilot was responsible.

In contrast, the NTSC's final report, published in December 2000, did not reach a definitive conclusion regarding the cause of the crash. The NTSC acknowledged the NTSB's findings but stated that there was insufficient evidence to determine whether the crash was caused by intentional actions or a mechanical failure. The NTSC's report emphasized the lack of conclusive evidence and highlighted the need for further investigation into potential mechanical issues.

The differing conclusions of the NTSC and the NTSB led to significant controversy and debate within the aviation community and among the victims' families. The ambiguity surrounding the cause of the crash left many questions unanswered and fueled speculation about the true events leading up to the disaster. Some independent analysts and experts suggested alternative theories, including potential mechanical failures, uncommanded rudder movements, or other unexplained anomalies. However, none of these theories were conclusively proven.

The crash of SilkAir Flight 185 had profound implications for aviation safety and regulatory practices. In response to the NTSB's findings, the FAA and other aviation authorities implemented several measures to enhance cockpit security and monitoring. These measures included:

1. **Enhanced Cockpit Security**: Airlines and aviation regulators introduced stricter protocols to ensure that at least two authorized personnel were present in the cockpit at all times. This measure aimed to prevent unauthorized actions and ensure oversight of flight crew activities.

2. **Advanced Flight Data Monitoring**: The aviation industry adopted more sophisticated flight data monitoring systems to track and analyze pilot actions and aircraft performance in real time. These systems provided early warning of unusual behavior and allowed for more effective post-incident analysis.

3. **Improved Crew Resource Management (CRM) Training**: Training programs for pilots and flight crews were revised to emphasize teamwork, communication, and decision-making skills. CRM training aimed to enhance the ability of flight

crews to work together effectively and manage complex situations.

4. **Psychological Screening and Support**: Airlines introduced more comprehensive psychological screening and support programs for pilots and flight crew members. These programs aimed to identify and address potential mental health issues, stress, or other factors that could impact performance.

5. **Enhanced Flight Recorder Technology**: Advances in flight recorder technology were implemented to ensure more robust and reliable data capture. This included improvements to the durability and data retention capabilities of CVRs and FDRs, as well as the development of additional data recording systems.

The legacy of SilkAir Flight 185 is marked by the tragedy of the loss of 104 lives and the ongoing quest for understanding and closure. Memorials were established to honor the victims, including a permanent memorial at the crash site near Palembang. The crash also served as a reminder of the critical importance of aviation safety and the need for continuous improvement in safety practices, training, and technology.

The unresolved nature of the crash continues to be a source of debate and reflection within the aviation community. While the NTSB's conclusion points to deliberate actions by a crewmember, the lack of definitive evidence and the conflicting findings of the NTSC highlight the complexities and challenges involved in aviation accident investigations. The lessons learned from SilkAir Flight 185 have contributed to ongoing efforts to enhance safety, prevent similar tragedies, and ensure the highest standards of accountability and transparency in aviation.

The story of SilkAir Flight 185 is a poignant reminder of the fragility of human life and the relentless pursuit of safety and excellence in aviation. It underscores the importance of rigorous investigation, open dialogue, and continuous innovation in making air travel as safe as possible for all.

Chapter 19: Helios Airways Flight 522

Helios Airways Flight 522 was a scheduled passenger flight from Larnaca, Cyprus, to Prague, Czech Republic, with a stopover in Athens, Greece. On August 14, 2005, the flight met a tragic end, resulting in one of the most baffling and eerie aviation disasters in history. This incident, often referred to as the "Ghost Plane," captivated the world and highlighted critical issues in aviation safety protocols.

The Boeing 737-31S aircraft, registered as 5B-DBY, took off from Larnaca at 09:07 local time. The initial stages of the flight were routine, but soon after takeoff, the crew reported a problem with the aircraft's cooling system. The Helios maintenance team on the ground was contacted, and they advised the crew to check the circuit breaker for the cooling system. This was the last communication from the aircraft.

As the plane ascended to its cruising altitude, it began to follow its programmed flight path. However, the pressurization system was not set correctly, leading to a gradual loss of cabin pressure. The crew, Captain Hans-Jürgen Merten and First Officer Pampos Charalambous, along with the passengers, began to suffer from hypoxia—oxygen deprivation. This condition can cause confusion, unconsciousness, and ultimately death if not rectified quickly.

Aboard the aircraft were 115 passengers, mostly Cypriot families and 6 crew members. As the plane continued on autopilot, it maintained its cruising altitude, oblivious to the emergency unfolding inside. The flight entered Greek airspace without making contact with air traffic control, raising concerns among controllers.

The Greek Air Force scrambled two F-16 fighter jets to intercept the unresponsive aircraft. When the fighter pilots approached Flight 522, they observed a chilling sight: the aircraft was flying normally, but the pilots appeared slumped over the controls. The passenger oxygen masks had deployed, indicating a cabin depressurization. The fighter pilots tried to establish visual contact, but there was no response from inside the cockpit.

One of the most haunting details was the sight of a flight attendant, Andreas Prodromou, who was also a trained pilot, attempting to regain control of the aircraft. Wearing an oxygen mask, he managed to enter the cockpit, but his efforts were in vain. The aircraft continued to fly on autopilot until it ran out of fuel. At 12:04 local time, Flight 522 crashed into a hillside near Grammatiko, Greece, killing all 121 people on board.

The subsequent investigation by the Hellenic Air Accident Investigation and Aviation Safety Board (AAIASB) revealed several critical factors leading to the disaster. The primary cause was identified as the incorrect setting of the pressurization mode selector, which was left in the manual position instead of the automatic position after a maintenance check. This oversight led to the cabin not being pressurized as the aircraft climbed, causing the gradual hypoxia that incapacitated the crew and passengers.

The investigation also highlighted deficiencies in Helios Airways' maintenance and operational procedures. The airline had a history of safety issues and was criticized for inadequate training and oversight of its maintenance staff. The report underscored the importance of proper maintenance protocols and the need for rigorous checks and balances to prevent such tragedies.

Moreover, the incident brought to light the critical role of effective communication and situational awareness in aviation. The crew's failure to recognize and respond to the pressurization problem in a timely manner was a key factor in the disaster. The lack of a coherent emergency response plan exacerbated the situation, as the crew's actions were disjointed and ineffective under the stress of hypoxia.

In the aftermath of the crash, several recommendations were made to improve aviation safety. These included enhancements to crew training, particularly in recognizing and responding to pressurization issues, and stricter oversight of airline maintenance practices. The importance of automated systems and alerts was also emphasized, ensuring that such critical errors would be promptly identified and corrected in the future.

Helios Airways ceased operations in 2006, a year after the crash, as the airline struggled to recover from the negative publicity and financial losses. The legacy of Flight 522 serves as a stark reminder of the devastating consequences of seemingly minor oversights and the vital importance of adherence to safety protocols in aviation.

The story of Helios Airways Flight 522 remains one of the most haunting aviation disasters. It is a testament to the critical need for vigilance, rigorous training, and robust safety measures in the complex and unforgiving realm of air travel. The tragedy not only marked a dark day in aviation history but also spurred important changes aimed at preventing similar incidents in the future.

Chapter 20: China Airlines Flight 611

China Airlines Flight 611, a scheduled international flight from Taipei, Taiwan to Hong Kong, met a tragic end on May 25, 2002. This disaster, resulting in the loss of all 225 passengers and crew members aboard, is a significant case study in aviation safety, illustrating the catastrophic potential of undetected structural damage and the critical importance of rigorous maintenance protocols.

The aircraft involved was a Boeing 747-209B, registered as B-18255, which had been in service since 1979. The flight, which departed from Chiang Kai-shek International Airport (now Taiwan Taoyuan International Airport) at 15:08 local time, was initially routine. The plane was to climb to its cruising altitude of 35,000 feet for the short journey to Hong Kong International Airport.

The sequence of events leading to the crash began nearly 22 years prior to the incident. On February 7, 1980, the same aircraft had suffered a tailstrike during a landing at Kai Tak Airport in Hong Kong. A tailstrike occurs when the tail of the aircraft hits the runway during landing or takeoff. This incident caused significant structural damage to the lower aft fuselage of the aircraft. Although repairs were made, they were not conducted in accordance with Boeing's prescribed procedures. The improper repair involved an inadequate splice plate, which did not restore the full structural integrity of the fuselage.

The inadequate repair left a latent defect in the aircraft's structure, which would become critical over time due to the stresses and strains experienced during normal flight operations. Despite undergoing regular maintenance checks, the defect went undetected for more than two decades.

On the day of the flight, the aircraft reached its cruising altitude and continued on its flight path. At approximately 16:16 local time, the aircraft was flying over the Taiwan Strait when it suddenly disintegrated in mid-air. Radar data showed that the aircraft rapidly lost altitude, and debris was scattered over a wide area of the sea.

The investigation into the crash, led by the Aviation Safety Council (ASC) of Taiwan, revealed that the aircraft had broken up due to a structural failure in the lower aft fuselage, precisely at the site of the improper repair made in 1980. The compromised structural integrity had finally succumbed to metal fatigue, leading to catastrophic failure. The pressurized cabin experienced explosive decompression, causing the aircraft to break apart almost instantly.

Further analysis showed that the fuselage's failure had been progressive, with fatigue cracks propagating over time. These cracks were not detected during routine maintenance checks, largely because the inspections were not comprehensive enough to identify such deep-seated structural issues. The inadequacy of the inspection protocols at the time allowed the fatal defect to remain unnoticed.

In addition to the structural failure, the investigation highlighted several other contributing factors. The primary one was the failure to adhere to proper repair procedures following the 1980 tailstrike. Boeing's recommended repair process involved a much more extensive reinforcement of the damaged area, which would have restored the necessary strength to the aircraft's structure. The substandard repair work performed at that time left the aircraft vulnerable to the eventual failure that occurred.

The investigation also revealed deficiencies in the regulatory oversight and maintenance practices of China Airlines. The airline's maintenance program did not adequately account for the long-term effects of previous damage, and their inspections were not thorough enough to detect the growing cracks. This pointed to a broader issue within the airline's safety culture and maintenance procedures.

The aftermath of the crash led to significant changes in aviation safety regulations and practices. The ASC and international aviation authorities, including the Federal Aviation Administration (FAA) and

Boeing, issued directives to ensure more stringent inspection and repair protocols. These included mandatory inspections of older aircraft, particularly focusing on areas that had previously sustained damage and undergone repairs.

China Airlines faced intense scrutiny and criticism for its maintenance practices and overall safety standards. The airline undertook a comprehensive review of its maintenance procedures and implemented substantial reforms to enhance its safety protocols. This included more rigorous training for maintenance personnel, improved inspection techniques, and closer adherence to manufacturers' repair guidelines.

The disaster of China Airlines Flight 611 also underscored the importance of transparent and thorough record-keeping. Accurate and detailed maintenance records are crucial for tracking the history of repairs and inspections, allowing for better identification of potential vulnerabilities. The incident prompted the aviation industry to place greater emphasis on meticulous documentation and proactive measures to identify and rectify latent defects.

In addition to regulatory and procedural changes, the crash had a profound impact on the families of the victims and the broader community. Memorials and tributes were established to honor the memory of those who lost their lives, serving as a somber reminder of the human cost of aviation accidents. The tragedy also fostered a deeper understanding of the importance of aviation safety among the public and within the industry.

The legacy of China Airlines Flight 611 is one of learning and improvement. The disaster highlighted the need for constant vigilance in aircraft maintenance and the critical importance of adhering to proper repair protocols. It served as a catalyst for positive changes in the aviation industry, driving advancements in safety standards and practices to prevent similar tragedies in the future.

Chapter 21: Indian Airlines Flight 814

Indian Airlines Flight 814, commonly known as IC 814, became one of the most infamous hijackings in aviation history. The incident, which occurred in December 1999, involved a passenger aircraft hijacked en route from Tribhuvan International Airport in Kathmandu, Nepal, to Indira Gandhi International Airport in New Delhi, India. The hijacking unfolded over several days and multiple countries, ending in a dramatic and controversial rescue operation.

On December 24, 1999, IC 814, an Airbus A300B2-101 registered VT-EDW, took off from Kathmandu with 176 passengers and 15 crew members aboard. The flight was expected to be routine, but it turned into a nightmare when, shortly after entering Indian airspace, five armed hijackers seized control of the aircraft. The hijackers, later identified as members of the Islamist militant group Harkat-ul-Mujahideen, were equipped with knives, pistols, and grenades. They quickly subdued the crew and announced their demands, which included the release of militants held in Indian prisons and a ransom of $200 million.

The hijackers forced the aircraft to divert from its planned route, initially attempting to land in Lahore, Pakistan. Pakistani authorities, however, denied permission to land, prompting the hijackers to fly to Amritsar in Punjab, India. Indian authorities were caught off guard by the hijacking, and their response at Amritsar was criticized for being slow and disorganized. The aircraft was refueled, but no decisive action was taken to end the hijacking. This allowed the hijackers to take off again, heading towards Lahore once more.

After being denied landing rights in Pakistan again, the aircraft was rerouted to Dubai in the United Arab Emirates. During the stopover in Dubai, the hijackers released 27 passengers, including women and children, as a gesture of goodwill. Despite this partial release, the situation remained tense, with the remaining hostages' lives hanging in the balance.

From Dubai, the aircraft was directed to Kandahar in Afghanistan, then under the control of the Taliban. The Taliban, known for their extremist rule, offered to mediate between the hijackers and the Indian government. The plane landed in Kandahar on December 25, and the hijackers established a standoff that would last for several days.

The Indian government, led by Prime Minister Atal Bihari Vajpayee, faced immense pressure to resolve the crisis. The hijackers' demands included the release of three prominent militants: Maulana Masood Azhar, the founder of Jaish-e-Mohammed; Ahmed Omar Saeed Sheikh, who later gained notoriety for his involvement in the kidnapping and murder of journalist Daniel Pearl; and Mushtaq Ahmed Zargar, a Kashmiri militant. The Indian authorities were initially reluctant to accede to these demands, fearing the release of such dangerous individuals would have severe repercussions for national security.

Throughout the standoff, the conditions on the aircraft deteriorated. The hostages were subjected to extreme stress, and there were growing concerns about their health and safety. The hijackers maintained a threatening demeanor, and the possibility of violence loomed large. The Indian government sent a negotiating team to Kandahar, which included diplomats and intelligence officers. The negotiators faced a complex situation, balancing the need to secure the hostages' release with the imperative to avoid empowering terrorist groups through concessions.

On December 31, 1999, after several rounds of intense negotiations, the Indian government made the difficult decision to agree to the hijackers' demands. The three militants were flown to Kandahar and handed over to the Taliban, who then facilitated their release to the hijackers. In exchange, all the remaining hostages were freed, and the hijackers were allowed to leave Kandahar unscathed. The Airbus A300 was subsequently returned to Indian authorities.

The resolution of the hijacking was met with a mixture of relief and outrage. While the safe return of the hostages was celebrated, the release of dangerous militants sparked widespread criticism and concern. Many feared that the concession would embolden terrorist groups and lead to further attacks. These fears were not unfounded, as Maulana Masood Azhar went on to play a key role in organizing several high-profile terrorist attacks in India, including the 2001 Indian Parliament attack and the 2019 Pulwama attack.

The IC 814 hijacking had far-reaching implications for Indian national security policy and counter-terrorism strategies. The incident exposed significant gaps in India's ability to respond to such crises, leading to a comprehensive review and overhaul of aviation security protocols. Measures were implemented to enhance airport security, including stricter screening procedures and improved coordination among security agencies. The government also established the National Security Guard's (NSG) Special Action Group to specifically deal with hijackings and other critical situations.

Internationally, the hijacking highlighted the complexities of dealing with state-sponsored terrorism and the challenges of negotiating with non-state actors operating across borders. The role of the Taliban in facilitating the hijackers' demands underscored the difficulties of addressing terrorism emanating from failed or unrecognized states.

The legacy of the IC 814 hijacking continues to influence India's security policies. The government's experience during this crisis has informed its approach to subsequent terrorist incidents, emphasizing a more robust and proactive stance against terrorism. The incident also reinforced the need for international cooperation in combating terrorism, leading to stronger diplomatic efforts to address the issue at global forums.

In the years following the hijacking, several of the key figures involved have faced justice. Ahmed Omar Saeed Sheikh was arrested in Pakistan in 2002 and sentenced to death for his role in the Daniel Pearl kidnapping, though his sentence was later commuted. Maulana Masood Azhar remains a prominent militant leader, and efforts to sanction him as a global terrorist have been pursued at the United Nations.

The IC 814 hijacking remains a pivotal event in the history of aviation terrorism. It serves as a stark reminder of the vulnerability of civilian aircraft to terrorist attacks and the profound impact such incidents can have on national security and public consciousness. The bravery of the passengers and crew, the complex negotiations, and the difficult decisions made by the Indian government during those harrowing days continue to be studied as critical lessons in crisis management and counter-terrorism.

Chapter 22: Air India Express Flight 812

Air India Express Flight 812 was one of the deadliest aviation disasters in Indian history, occurring on May 22, 2010. The flight was a scheduled international service from Dubai, United Arab Emirates, to Mangalore, India. Tragically, the aircraft overran the runway upon landing and crashed, resulting in the deaths of 158 out of 166 people on board. This incident highlighted critical issues in aviation safety, runway operations, and pilot training.

The aircraft involved was a Boeing 737-800, registered as VT-AXV. It departed from Dubai International Airport at 01:06 local time with 160 passengers and six crew members. The flight was commanded by Captain Zlatko Glušica, a Serbian national with over 10,000 flight hours, and First Officer Harbinder Singh Ahluwalia, an experienced pilot with over 3,500 flight hours. The journey was largely uneventful until the final approach into Mangalore's Bajpe Airport, which has a table-top runway situated on a plateau surrounded by deep gorges.

As the aircraft approached Mangalore, the weather was reported to be fair, with light rain and moderate visibility. The airport's runway 24, where the landing was to be executed, is known for its challenging approach due to its short length of 8,033 feet and its location atop a hill with steep drop-offs at both ends. This requires precise landing techniques, particularly in adverse weather conditions.

The final approach began with the aircraft aligning with the runway at an appropriate descent rate. However, critical errors soon unfolded. Captain Glušica, who was the pilot flying, had reportedly been awake for over 24 hours before the flight and was suffering from fatigue, a significant factor that would affect his performance. During the descent, the aircraft was above the recommended glide path, and the crew received multiple Ground Proximity Warning System (GPWS) alerts signaling that the descent was too rapid and the altitude was too high.

Despite these warnings, Captain Glušica did not execute a go-around, a standard procedure when an approach is not stable. Instead, he continued with the landing attempt, resulting in the aircraft touching down approximately 5,200 feet down the runway, far beyond the usual touchdown zone. This left insufficient runway length for the aircraft to come to a safe stop.

Upon touchdown, the crew applied the brakes and attempted to deploy the speed brakes and thrust reversers, but the aircraft was already traveling too fast to stop within the remaining runway. The plane overshot the runway end, broke through the airport perimeter fence, and plunged into the ravine at the end of the runway. The impact caused the aircraft to break apart and catch fire.

The crash site was located in a difficult-to-access area, complicating rescue operations. However, local villagers and airport rescue teams responded swiftly, managing to rescue eight survivors from the wreckage. These survivors were seated in the front section of the aircraft, which remained relatively intact compared to the rear sections that were destroyed by the impact and subsequent fire.

The aftermath of the crash saw extensive investigations conducted by the Directorate General of Civil Aviation (DGCA) of India, along with assistance from international aviation safety agencies such as the National Transportation Safety Board (NTSB) of the United States and Boeing. The investigation focused on several key areas, including the human factors involved, the aircraft's mechanical condition, and the airport's infrastructure.

The final investigation report revealed that pilot error was the primary cause of the crash. Captain Glušica's fatigue and his failure to follow standard operating procedures were cited as critical factors. His decision to continue the landing despite clear indications that the approach was unstable and his subsequent failure to execute a go-around were pivotal errors. Additionally, the report highlighted systemic issues such as inadequate crew resource management (CRM), where the First Officer did not effectively intervene or challenge the Captain's decisions, possibly due to hierarchical dynamics and cultural factors.

The investigation also noted that while the aircraft was in good mechanical condition, there were lapses in cockpit discipline and adherence to procedural protocols. These included ignoring multiple GPWS alerts and failing to execute a go-around. The role of fatigue was particularly emphasized, pointing to the need for stricter enforcement of duty time regulations and better fatigue management practices among flight crew.

In response to the findings, several safety recommendations were made to prevent similar accidents in the future. These included enhancing pilot training programs with a greater focus on CRM, emphasizing the importance of go-around procedures, and addressing the issue of pilot fatigue through better scheduling practices and monitoring. The DGCA also recommended improvements in airport infrastructure, particularly at table-top runways like Mangalore, which pose unique challenges.

Additionally, the crash prompted a broader discussion on aviation safety culture in India. It underscored the need for a more proactive approach to safety management, including regular audits of airline operations and stricter enforcement of safety regulations. The importance of creating an environment where co-pilots feel empowered to speak up and challenge decisions when necessary was also highlighted.

The tragic event of Air India Express Flight 812 also had a profound impact on the families of the victims and the broader community. Memorials and tributes were established to honor the memory of those who lost their lives, and efforts were made to provide support and compensation to the families affected by the disaster. The incident remains etched in the collective memory of the Indian aviation community and serves as a poignant reminder of the critical importance of safety and vigilance in aviation.

In the years following the crash, Air India Express and other Indian carriers have worked to implement the recommendations made by the investigation authorities. These efforts have included upgrading flight simulators, enhancing training programs, and fostering a safety-first culture within the organization. The airline has also engaged in continuous dialogue with regulatory bodies to ensure compliance with international safety standards.

The legacy of Air India Express Flight 812 continues to influence aviation safety practices in India and globally. The lessons learned from this tragic event have contributed to a deeper understanding of the human factors involved in aviation accidents and the importance of robust safety management systems. The incident serves as a sobering reminder of the complexities and risks inherent in aviation and the ongoing need for vigilance, discipline, and continuous improvement in safety practices.

Chapter 23: Aeroflot Flight 593

Aeroflot Flight 593 was a passenger flight from Sheremetyevo International Airport in Moscow, Russia, to Kai Tak Airport in Hong Kong, which crashed into a mountainside in the Kuznetsk Alatau mountain range of Siberia on March 23, 1994. The disaster resulted in the deaths of all 75 people on board. The cause of the crash was an unusual and tragic set of circumstances involving pilot error and the unintended deactivation of the autopilot by an untrained person in the cockpit.

The aircraft involved was an Airbus A310-304, registration F-OGQS, operated by Aeroflot – Russian International Airlines, the international subsidiary of Aeroflot. The captain of the flight was Andrey Viktorovich Danilov, an experienced pilot with extensive flight hours, and the first officer was Yaroslav Vladimirovich Kudrinsky, who had significant flying experience as well. However, what made this flight unique and ultimately catastrophic were the unplanned actions involving Kudrinsky's children, who were present in the cockpit during the flight.

The flight began uneventfully, taking off from Moscow at 16:39 UTC. The aircraft climbed to its cruising altitude of 33,000 feet, and the flight crew settled into routine operations as the aircraft cruised towards its destination. The cockpit was equipped with modern avionics, including an autopilot system designed to handle most aspects of flight management once the aircraft was airborne.

During the cruise phase, First Officer Kudrinsky invited his children, 16-year-old Eldar and 12-year-old Yana, into the cockpit, a common practice at the time, especially on Aeroflot flights, which had more lenient cockpit protocols than Western airlines. Kudrinsky allowed his children to sit in the captain's seat and handle the controls briefly, under his supervision, to give them a feel of what it was like to pilot an aircraft.

At approximately 05:40 local time, Eldar was seated in the captain's seat, and Kudrinsky, standing behind him, allowed Eldar to manipulate the control column. Unknown to the crew, when Eldar applied a minor input to the control column, the autopilot partially disconnected from maintaining the ailerons, which control the aircraft's roll. This mode of partial disconnection did not alert the crew with a noticeable alarm, and the aircraft began to gradually bank to the right.

Initially, the change was subtle, but as the bank angle increased, the aircraft began a slow roll. The autopilot, still controlling the elevator and thrust, attempted to maintain altitude, leading to a gradual but unnoticed increase in the roll angle. When the bank angle reached 45 degrees, the autopilot fully disconnected, an event that did trigger a warning chime. At this point, the aircraft was in a steepening right bank and descending.

The crew's reaction to the situation was delayed as they tried to comprehend the sudden loss of autopilot control. Captain Danilov and First Officer Kudrinsky took immediate actions to try to regain control of the aircraft. However, the increasing bank angle and the descent created a high-stress scenario that led to confusion and disorientation.

As the aircraft continued to descend rapidly, it reached a bank angle of nearly 90 degrees, effectively putting it into a near-inverted position. The rapid descent increased the speed, and the crew's attempts to level the wings and arrest the descent were not successful due to the severe disorientation and the complexity of the situation.

At 05:49 local time, after a chaotic and desperate struggle to regain control, the aircraft crashed into a remote hillside in the Kuznetsk Alatau mountain range. The impact was catastrophic, and there were no survivors. The wreckage was scattered over a wide area, making recovery operations challenging.

The investigation into the crash was conducted by the Russian Federation's Interstate Aviation Committee (MAK), with assistance from Airbus and other international aviation safety agencies. The cockpit voice recorder (CVR) and flight data recorder (FDR) were recovered from the crash site, providing crucial insights into the final moments of the flight.

The analysis of the flight recorders confirmed that the crash was precipitated by the accidental deactivation of the autopilot's roll control by Eldar, the First Officer's son. The subsequent chain of events, including the lack of immediate recognition of the autopilot's disengagement and the delayed response to the increasingly critical flight attitude, led to the fatal descent.

The investigation also highlighted several contributing factors, including the absence of clear visual or auditory warnings to the crew when the autopilot partially disconnected and the inadequate response protocols for such a situation. Furthermore, the presence of untrained individuals in the cockpit and their interaction with the aircraft's controls was a significant deviation from standard operating procedures.

In response to the findings, Aeroflot and the broader aviation community took several measures to prevent similar incidents in the future. These included stricter enforcement of cockpit protocols, prohibiting unauthorized persons from handling flight controls, and improvements in autopilot design to ensure more explicit warnings and fail-safes when partial disconnections occur.

Additionally, the incident underscored the importance of crew resource management (CRM) training, which emphasizes communication, decision-making, and situational awareness among flight crew members. Enhanced CRM training programs were developed to better prepare pilots for handling unexpected and unusual situations effectively.

The crash of Aeroflot Flight 593 also led to broader regulatory changes within the aviation industry. The International Civil Aviation Organization (ICAO) and other regulatory bodies introduced more stringent regulations regarding cockpit access and the interaction of non-crew members with aircraft controls during flight.

The legacy of Aeroflot Flight 593 is a sobering reminder of the critical importance of adhering to established safety protocols and the potentially dire consequences of even seemingly minor deviations. The incident remains a case study in aviation safety, highlighting the complex interplay between human factors, technology, and procedural compliance in ensuring the safe operation of commercial aircraft.

In the aftermath of the tragedy, memorials were established to honor the victims, and efforts were made to support the families affected by the disaster. The lessons learned from this incident have continued to influence aviation safety practices and have contributed to the development of more robust safety cultures within airlines around the world.

The story of Aeroflot Flight 593 is a poignant example of how unforeseen and unusual factors can lead to catastrophic outcomes in aviation. It underscores the need for constant vigilance, rigorous adherence to safety procedures, and continuous improvement in training and technology to ensure the safety of air travel.

Chapter 24: Delta Air Lines Flight 191

Delta Air Lines Flight 191, a scheduled passenger flight from Fort Lauderdale, Florida, to Los Angeles, California, with a stopover in Dallas/Fort Worth International Airport, became the focus of one of the most significant aviation disaster investigations in history due to its tragic crash on August 2, 1985. This accident highlighted critical issues related to microburst-induced wind shear, weather radar technology, and pilot training, leading to widespread changes in aviation safety protocols and procedures.

The aircraft involved was a Lockheed L-1011-385-1 TriStar, registration N726DA. It was a wide-body, three-engine jetliner with an excellent safety record, capable of carrying 274 passengers. On this fateful day, the flight was piloted by Captain Edward Connors, First Officer Rudolph Price, and Flight Engineer Nick Nassick. The flight crew, like the aircraft, had commendable records and extensive experience.

Flight 191 departed from Fort Lauderdale at 14:10 EDT and was scheduled to arrive at Dallas/Fort Worth International Airport (DFW) at around 17:45 CDT. The weather en route was generally good, but conditions near Dallas were deteriorating. As the aircraft approached DFW, a line of thunderstorms had developed north of the airport, producing conditions ripe for severe weather, including the deadly phenomenon known as a microburst, which would soon play a central role in the disaster.

A microburst is a localized column of sinking air within a thunderstorm, leading to a powerful downdraft that hits the ground and spreads out in all directions. This can create rapid changes in wind speed and direction over a very short distance, known as wind shear, which can be extremely hazardous to aircraft, especially during takeoff and landing phases when they are at lower altitudes and speeds.

At 17:43, Flight 191 began its final approach to runway 17L at DFW. The air traffic controller provided weather updates, noting the presence of thunderstorms and rain showers near the airport. Despite these warnings, the crew decided to continue the approach. At approximately 17:45, the aircraft entered a region of turbulence, and the crew noticed a rain shaft ahead, indicating the presence of a thunderstorm. The plane continued its descent, and the pilots maintained communication with the tower, acknowledging the weather information and preparing for a landing.

At around 17:47, the aircraft encountered a sudden and severe downdraft, part of a microburst. The wind shear conditions rapidly worsened, causing significant changes in airspeed and altitude. Initially, the aircraft experienced a headwind, which increased its airspeed. This was followed almost immediately by a powerful tailwind, which decreased airspeed and reduced lift. The flight crew struggled to control the aircraft, applying full power to the engines in an attempt to climb out of the microburst, but it was too late.

The L-1011 descended rapidly, and at 17:48, it struck a car on Texas State Highway 114, which runs adjacent to the airport. The impact killed the driver and destroyed a light pole. The aircraft then struck two water tanks on the airport property, causing it to break apart and burst into flames. Of the 163 people on board, 136 passengers and 8 crew members were killed. Remarkably, 27 people survived, including the Flight Engineer, Nick Nassick, who sustained serious injuries but lived.

The aftermath of the crash saw a massive response from emergency services, who worked tirelessly to rescue survivors and manage the chaotic scene. The National Transportation Safety Board (NTSB) quickly launched an investigation to determine the causes of the accident and prevent similar incidents in the future. The investigation revealed critical insights into the dangers of microbursts and the challenges they pose to aviation safety.

The NTSB's final report, released in 1986, identified the primary cause of the crash as the flight crew's inability to recognize and respond effectively to the wind shear conditions. The investigation highlighted several key factors, including the limitations of the weather radar technology available at the time, which was not capable of detecting microbursts. Additionally, the report criticized the lack of adequate pilot training on how to handle microburst-induced wind shear.

One significant finding was that the onboard weather radar used by the crew was not sophisticated enough to detect the microburst. This limitation meant that the pilots were flying into a dangerous situation without full awareness of the severity of the weather conditions. The NTSB also pointed out that the existing wind shear detection systems at airports were inadequate for providing timely and accurate warnings to pilots.

The report made several recommendations aimed at improving aviation safety. These included the development and deployment of more advanced wind shear detection and alert systems, enhancements in pilot training programs to better prepare crews for encountering microbursts, and improvements in weather radar technology. The NTSB also recommended changes to air traffic control procedures to ensure that pilots receive timely and accurate weather information.

In response to these recommendations, significant advancements were made in aviation safety technology and procedures. The Federal Aviation Administration (FAA) and other aviation authorities around the world invested in the development and installation of Terminal Doppler Weather Radar (TDWR) systems at major airports. These systems are capable of detecting microbursts and providing real-time warnings to air traffic controllers and pilots, significantly enhancing their ability to avoid dangerous wind shear conditions.

Pilot training programs were also overhauled to include comprehensive training on wind shear recognition and recovery techniques. Simulators were updated to incorporate realistic wind shear scenarios, allowing pilots to practice and refine their responses to such conditions. This training became a mandatory part of pilot certification and recurrent training programs, ensuring that flight crews are better prepared to handle the challenges posed by microbursts.

Furthermore, aircraft manufacturers developed and implemented advanced onboard wind shear detection and alert systems. These systems use data from multiple sensors to detect rapid changes in wind speed and direction, providing pilots with timely warnings and guidance on how to respond. The introduction of these systems has significantly improved the ability of pilots to detect and respond to wind shear, reducing the risk of accidents.

The legacy of Delta Air Lines Flight 191 extends beyond the technological and procedural improvements it spurred. The crash served as a stark reminder of the importance of respecting weather hazards and the need for continuous improvement in aviation safety. The lessons learned from this tragedy have been instrumental in shaping modern aviation practices and ensuring that the industry remains vigilant in addressing emerging safety challenges.

In the years following the crash, aviation authorities and organizations have continued to build on the advancements prompted by the Flight 191 investigation. Collaborative efforts between meteorologists, engineers, and pilots have led to a deeper understanding of microburst dynamics and the development of even more sophisticated detection and response technologies. These ongoing efforts reflect the industry's commitment to learning from past accidents and preventing future tragedies.

Delta Air Lines Flight 191 remains a somber chapter in aviation history, but it also stands as a testament to the resilience and dedication of the aviation community in the face of adversity. The improvements in weather detection technology, pilot training, and safety protocols that emerged from the investigation have undoubtedly saved lives and made air travel safer for everyone.

The memory of those who lost their lives in the crash continues to inspire a relentless pursuit of excellence in aviation safety. Memorials and tributes to the victims serve as poignant reminders of the human cost of complacency and the enduring need for vigilance and innovation. As the aviation industry looks to the future, the lessons of Delta Air Lines Flight 191 remain a guiding force, shaping a safer and more resilient air travel environment for generations to come.

Chapter 25: Alaska Airlines Flight 261

Alaska Airlines Flight 261 was a scheduled domestic passenger flight from Lic. Gustavo Díaz Ordaz International Airport in Puerto Vallarta, Mexico, to Seattle-Tacoma International Airport in Seattle, Washington, with an intermediate stop at San Francisco International Airport in San Francisco, California. On January 31, 2000, the flight crashed into the Pacific Ocean off the coast of California, near Anacapa Island, killing all 88 people on board. This tragedy brought significant attention to aircraft maintenance practices and the importance of adhering to stringent safety standards.

The aircraft involved was a McDonnell Douglas MD-83, a popular medium-range, twin-engine jetliner. The aircraft was registered as N963AS and had been in service since 1992. It had accumulated approximately 26,584 flight hours and 14,315 cycles (a cycle is defined as one takeoff and landing). The flight was commanded by Captain Ted Thompson, a highly experienced pilot with 17,750 flight hours, and First Officer William "Bill" Tansky, who had 8,140 flight hours. Both pilots were well-regarded professionals with extensive experience flying the MD-80 series aircraft.

Flight 261 departed Puerto Vallarta at 13:37 PST, bound for San Francisco. The first part of the flight was uneventful, and the crew maintained communication with air traffic control (ATC) while cruising at 31,000 feet. Approximately two hours into the flight, the pilots began to experience difficulty controlling the aircraft's horizontal stabilizer, a critical component of the tailplane responsible for adjusting the aircraft's pitch.

The horizontal stabilizer is adjusted via a jackscrew mechanism, which moves the entire stabilizer up or down to change the angle of the aircraft's nose. This jackscrew is lubricated to prevent excessive wear and ensure smooth operation. During the flight, the crew reported that they were having difficulty trimming the aircraft's stabilizer, indicating that it was not responding correctly to inputs. This issue had surfaced intermittently during the flight, but it became more pronounced as the aircraft continued its journey.

At 16:09 PST, the pilots contacted Alaska Airlines maintenance control to discuss the issue. They were instructed to follow the procedures outlined in the aircraft's manual, which included attempts to free the stabilizer by applying alternating nose-up and nose-down trim commands. Despite their efforts, the stabilizer remained jammed, and the aircraft began to experience significant control difficulties.

As the flight progressed, the situation deteriorated. At 16:19 PST, the crew declared an emergency and requested an immediate diversion to Los Angeles International Airport (LAX). ATC granted the request, and the aircraft began its descent. During this descent, the control problems worsened, and the crew struggled to maintain stable flight.

At 16:20 PST, while descending through 23,000 feet, the MD-83 suddenly pitched nose-down into a steep dive. The pilots managed to regain some control and leveled the aircraft at approximately 24,000 feet. However, just moments later, at 16:21 PST, the aircraft entered another uncontrolled dive. The final moments were chaotic as the pilots fought to save the aircraft and the passengers onboard. Unfortunately, the aircraft continued its plunge, ultimately crashing into the Pacific Ocean at high speed.

The impact was catastrophic, and the wreckage was scattered over a large area of the ocean floor, approximately 10 miles offshore. There were no survivors among the 88 occupants, which included 83 passengers and 5 crew members. The National Transportation Safety Board (NTSB) immediately launched an investigation to determine the cause of the crash and prevent future occurrences.

The investigation was one of the most extensive and complex in the history of aviation accidents. The NTSB, along with the Federal Aviation Administration (FAA), Alaska Airlines, McDonnell Douglas (now part of Boeing), and other experts, collaborated to piece together the sequence of events that led to the disaster. The recovery of the aircraft's flight data recorder (FDR) and cockpit voice recorder (CVR) was crucial in understanding the technical and human factors involved.

The FDR and CVR provided detailed information about the aircraft's performance and the crew's actions in the final moments of the flight. Analysis of the data revealed that the primary cause of the crash was a failure of the horizontal stabilizer trim system due to a lack of proper lubrication of the jackscrew assembly. The threads of the jackscrew and the corresponding nut were found to be severely worn, causing the jackscrew to become stripped and leading to a loss of control over the stabilizer.

The NTSB's investigation traced the maintenance records of the aircraft and discovered that the interval between lubrication of the jackscrew assembly had been extended from every 500 flight hours to every 2,500 flight hours. This change was approved by the FAA based on a recommendation from Alaska Airlines, which argued that the extension was justified by operational data. However, the investigation revealed that this extended interval was insufficient to prevent excessive wear on the jackscrew assembly.

Further examination of maintenance practices at Alaska Airlines uncovered systemic issues, including insufficient training for mechanics and inadequate oversight of maintenance procedures. The investigation found that the airline had failed to perform the necessary lubrication of the jackscrew assembly during several maintenance checks, leading to the progressive wear that ultimately caused the failure.

In its final report, the NTSB identified several contributing factors to the crash, including the inadequate lubrication intervals, insufficient training for maintenance personnel, and a lack of effective oversight by the FAA. The report highlighted the critical importance of adhering to manufacturer-recommended maintenance schedules and ensuring that all components, especially those critical to flight safety, are properly serviced.

The NTSB made several recommendations to improve aviation safety and prevent similar accidents in the future. These included stricter adherence to manufacturer maintenance guidelines, enhanced training programs for maintenance personnel, improved oversight by regulatory authorities, and the development of more reliable systems for monitoring the condition of critical aircraft components.

In response to the findings, the FAA implemented new regulations requiring airlines to adhere strictly to manufacturer-recommended maintenance intervals. The agency also enhanced its oversight of airline maintenance programs and increased the frequency and rigor of inspections. Airlines were required to review and update their maintenance practices to ensure compliance with the new standards.

Alaska Airlines undertook significant changes to address the issues identified in the investigation. The airline revamped its maintenance procedures, implemented more stringent training programs for its mechanics, and improved its internal oversight processes. These changes were aimed at restoring confidence in the airline's commitment to safety and ensuring that such a tragedy would not happen again.

The crash of Alaska Airlines Flight 261 also led to broader changes within the aviation industry. Manufacturers, airlines, and regulatory authorities around the world reviewed and updated their maintenance practices and oversight procedures. The incident underscored the need for constant vigilance in maintaining aircraft systems and highlighted the potential consequences of deviating from established maintenance protocols.

The legacy of Flight 261 extends beyond the technical and procedural improvements it spurred. The tragedy had a profound impact on the families of the victims, the aviation community, and the public at large. Memorials were established to honor the lives lost, and efforts were made to support the grieving families and provide them with the necessary resources to cope with their loss.

The lessons learned from this disaster have become a cornerstone of aviation safety culture, emphasizing the critical importance of meticulous maintenance practices and rigorous adherence to safety standards. The memory of the passengers and crew of Flight 261 continues to inspire ongoing efforts to enhance aviation safety and prevent similar tragedies.

Chapter 26: Gol Transportes Aéreos Flight 1907

Gol Transportes Aéreos Flight 1907 was a scheduled domestic passenger flight from Manaus to Rio de Janeiro, Brazil, with an intermediate stop in Brasília. On September 29, 2006, the flight, operated by a Boeing 737-8EH, collided mid-air with an Embraer Legacy 600 business jet over the Amazon rainforest, resulting in the deaths of all 154 people on board the Boeing 737. The incident marked one of the deadliest aviation disasters in Brazilian history and led to extensive investigations and reforms in aviation safety and air traffic control procedures.

The Boeing 737-8EH, registration PR-GTD, was relatively new, having been delivered to Gol Transportes Aéreos in September 2006. It was commanded by Captain Decio Chaves Junior, a seasoned pilot with 15,498 flight hours, and First Officer Thiago Jordan de Onorati, who had 3,981 flight hours. The aircraft departed Manaus at 15:35 BRT with 148 passengers and six crew members on board, bound for Brasília where it would make a scheduled stop before continuing to Rio de Janeiro.

Simultaneously, the Embraer Legacy 600 business jet, registration N600XL, operated by ExcelAire Service Inc., a U.S.-based company, was on its maiden delivery flight from the Embraer factory in São José dos Campos to the United States. It was crewed by American pilots Captain Joseph Lepore and First Officer Jan Paladino. The Legacy jet took off from São José dos Campos and was scheduled to make a refueling stop in Manaus before continuing to the United States.

At approximately 16:56 BRT, while cruising at 37,000 feet (FL370) in the same airway (UZ6), the two aircraft collided. The left winglet of the Legacy jet sliced through the fuselage of the Boeing 737, resulting in the catastrophic failure of the 737's structural integrity.

The Boeing 737 broke apart in mid-air, and the wreckage fell into dense rainforest below. All 154 people on board the Boeing were killed instantly. The Legacy jet, despite suffering significant damage, managed to stabilize, and the pilots executed an emergency landing at a Brazilian military airstrip, Cachimbo Airport, without any injuries to the seven occupants on board.

The aftermath of the collision triggered a large-scale search and rescue operation in the Amazon rainforest. The remote and dense terrain complicated recovery efforts, but over the following days, Brazilian military and rescue teams managed to locate and retrieve the bodies of the victims and the wreckage of the aircraft. The tragedy deeply affected Brazil, prompting a period of national mourning and a strong demand for accountability and answers regarding how such a disaster could have occurred.

The investigation into the accident was conducted by the Brazilian Aeronautical Accidents Investigation and Prevention Center (CENIPA), with assistance from the National Transportation Safety Board (NTSB) from the United States and other international aviation authorities. The inquiry focused on several critical aspects, including air traffic control procedures, aircraft navigation systems, and pilot actions leading up to the collision.

The investigation revealed a series of errors and systemic issues that contributed to the mid-air collision. Firstly, there was a critical failure in communication and coordination between the air traffic controllers and the flight crews. The Legacy jet was initially cleared to climb to FL370 for a segment of its journey. However, due to a series of miscommunications and errors, the aircraft remained at FL370 instead of descending to a lower altitude as it approached the collision point. The Boeing 737 was correctly maintaining its assigned altitude of FL370, which it shared with the Legacy jet due to this miscommunication.

The Legacy jet's transponder, which provides information about the aircraft's position and altitude to air traffic controllers and other aircraft, was found to be inoperative at the time of the collision. This failure meant that the Traffic Collision Avoidance System (TCAS), which warns pilots of potential mid-air collisions, was not functioning on the Legacy jet. Consequently, neither aircraft received a TCAS alert to avoid each other.

The investigation also highlighted deficiencies in the Brazilian air traffic control system, including understaffing, inadequate training, and reliance on outdated radar technology. These systemic issues contributed to the controllers' inability to accurately track and communicate with the aircraft in their airspace. Specifically, the air traffic controllers failed to notice the conflict in altitudes between the two aircraft and did not issue timely instructions to correct the situation.

The final report by CENIPA, released in December 2008, concluded that the primary causes of the collision were the failures in air traffic control and the inadvertent actions of the Legacy jet's flight crew. The report noted that the crew did not follow standard procedures for confirming altitude changes and failed to maintain proper communication with air traffic control. It also criticized the lack of redundancy and reliability in the Legacy jet's transponder system.

The report made several recommendations aimed at improving aviation safety and preventing similar accidents in the future. These included enhancing air traffic controller training, upgrading radar and communication systems, and enforcing stricter adherence to standard operating procedures for flight crews. Additionally, it recommended that aircraft manufacturers improve the reliability and redundancy of critical avionics systems such as transponders.

In the wake of the disaster, the Brazilian government and aviation authorities implemented significant reforms. Investments were made to modernize the country's air traffic control infrastructure, including the installation of advanced radar systems and the hiring and training of additional air traffic controllers. Brazil also strengthened its regulatory framework to ensure stricter oversight of air traffic control operations and pilot compliance with flight procedures.

The legal and criminal ramifications of the crash were extensive. The pilots of the Legacy jet, Joseph Lepore and Jan Paladino, faced charges of negligent homicide in Brazil, based on accusations that their actions contributed to the collision. After a lengthy legal process, they were convicted in absentia in 2011 and received suspended sentences. The case sparked significant debate and controversy, particularly regarding the fairness of holding the pilots criminally liable for what many aviation experts considered a systemic failure.

Gol Transportes Aéreos Flight 1907 had a profound impact on the global aviation community. The International Civil Aviation Organization (ICAO) and other aviation bodies reviewed and revised their standards for air traffic control procedures, pilot training, and communication protocols to address the issues highlighted by the crash. The incident underscored the importance of robust and reliable communication and tracking systems in ensuring the safety of air travel.

Memorials were established to honor the victims of the tragedy, and efforts were made to support their families. The crash of Flight 1907 remains a somber reminder of the complexities and challenges of aviation safety. It illustrates how multiple factors, including human error, technological failures, and systemic deficiencies, can converge to create a catastrophic event.

The legacy of Gol Transportes Aéreos Flight 1907 continues to influence aviation safety practices and regulations worldwide. The improvements in air traffic control technology, enhanced pilot training programs, and strengthened regulatory oversight that emerged from the lessons learned from this disaster have undoubtedly contributed to making air travel safer. The memory of those who lost their lives in this tragic accident serves as a constant reminder of the importance of vigilance, communication, and adherence to safety protocols in aviation.

Chapter 27: AeroPerú Flight 603

AeroPerú Flight 603 was a scheduled passenger flight from Miami International Airport in Miami, Florida, to Comodoro Arturo Merino Benítez International Airport in Santiago, Chile, with stopovers in Quito, Ecuador, and Lima, Peru. On October 2, 1996, the Boeing 757-23A operating this flight crashed into the Pacific Ocean shortly after taking off from Lima. All 70 people on board were killed. The accident is particularly notable for the series of tragic errors and the fundamental importance of proper aircraft maintenance.

The Boeing 757-23A, registration N52AW, was a twin-engine jetliner known for its reliability and safety record. On the night of the accident, the aircraft was crewed by Captain Eric Schreiber and First Officer David Fernández Revoredo. Captain Schreiber had amassed a total of 22,000 flight hours, with 1,833 hours on the Boeing 757. First Officer Fernández Revoredo had a total of 8,000 flight hours, with 719 hours on the 757. Both pilots were highly experienced and well-regarded.

Flight 603 departed from Miami International Airport and made its first stop in Quito without incident. After a brief layover, the flight continued to Lima, where it arrived in the late evening of October 1. The final leg of the journey was scheduled to take the aircraft to Santiago. The weather conditions in Lima were typical for the region, with clear skies and calm winds, posing no immediate challenges to the flight.

The aircraft took off from Lima at approximately 00:42 local time on October 2. Shortly after takeoff, the pilots encountered an array of anomalous and confusing instrument readings. The primary flight displays (PFDs) and other crucial flight instruments provided contradictory and inaccurate information, creating a situation of extreme uncertainty in the cockpit. The pilots were receiving multiple warnings from the aircraft's onboard systems, including "rudder ratio," "mach airspeed trim," and "overspeed" alerts.

The flight crew quickly realized that they were facing a serious issue, but the exact nature of the problem was unclear. They attempted to troubleshoot the situation by referencing their checklists and discussing potential solutions. Despite their efforts, the erratic behavior of the instruments persisted. The conflicting warnings and erroneous data made it extremely difficult for the pilots to determine the aircraft's true altitude, airspeed, and attitude.

Compounding the crisis, the cockpit voice recorder (CVR) captured the growing confusion and frustration of the pilots as they struggled to understand and resolve the situation. The CVR also recorded the sounds of the multiple alarms and warnings that continued to blare in the background, adding to the chaos in the cockpit. The pilots repeatedly communicated with air traffic control (ATC), seeking assistance and attempting to convey the severity of their predicament.

At 00:54, the flight crew declared an emergency, reporting that they were experiencing a serious instrumentation failure and requesting vectors for a return to Lima. ATC cleared the flight to return and began providing radar vectors to guide the aircraft back to the airport. However, the erroneous instrument readings made it exceedingly difficult for the pilots to follow these instructions accurately.

Unbeknownst to the pilots, the root cause of the instrumentation failure was a simple but catastrophic maintenance oversight. During routine maintenance conducted shortly before the flight, adhesive tape had been applied over the static ports on the lower fuselage of the aircraft. The static ports are critical components that measure the atmospheric pressure outside the aircraft, providing essential data to the airspeed indicators, altimeters, and vertical speed indicators. The failure to remove the tape after the maintenance work rendered these instruments unreliable.

As Flight 603 attempted to navigate back to Lima, the situation grew more dire. The inaccurate altitude and airspeed readings led to improper handling of the aircraft, causing it to oscillate between steep climbs and descents. The pilots, despite their extensive experience, were unable to stabilize the aircraft due to the erroneous data. The confusion and stress in the cockpit were palpable, as captured by the CVR.

At approximately 01:11, after nearly 30 minutes of struggling to control the aircraft, Flight 603 impacted the Pacific Ocean. The aircraft broke apart on impact, and all 70 occupants, including 61 passengers and 9 crew members, perished. The wreckage sank to the ocean floor, where it was later recovered by search and rescue teams.

The investigation into the crash of AeroPerú Flight 603 was conducted by the Comisión de Investigación de Accidentes de Aviación (CIAA) of Peru, with assistance from the National Transportation Safety Board (NTSB) of the United States and representatives from Boeing. The inquiry focused on determining the precise sequence of events that led to the crash and identifying the underlying causes.

Investigators quickly identified the adhesive tape over the static ports as the primary cause of the instrumentation failure. The tape had been applied by maintenance personnel during routine cleaning and polishing of the aircraft and had not been removed before the flight. This oversight resulted in the blockage of the static ports, leading to the erroneous readings from the aircraft's instruments.

The investigation revealed several critical lapses in the maintenance procedures and oversight at AeroPerú. The airline's maintenance protocols did not include a specific step to ensure the removal of tape or other obstructions from the static ports after cleaning. Additionally, there was a lack of effective supervision and quality control measures to verify the completion of maintenance tasks. These deficiencies allowed the error to go unnoticed, setting the stage for the disaster.

The final report by the CIAA highlighted the importance of adhering to established maintenance procedures and the need for rigorous oversight to prevent similar incidents. The report also emphasized the critical role of the static ports in providing accurate data to the flight instruments and the catastrophic consequences of their obstruction. Several recommendations were made to improve maintenance practices, including the implementation of more stringent quality control measures and enhanced training for maintenance personnel.

In response to the findings, AeroPerú and other airlines around the world reviewed and revised their maintenance procedures to ensure that similar oversights could not occur. The incident underscored the importance of meticulous attention to detail in aircraft maintenance and the potentially devastating impact of seemingly minor errors.

The crash of Flight 603 also had broader implications for the aviation industry. Regulatory authorities, including the International Civil Aviation Organization (ICAO) and national aviation agencies, took steps to enhance maintenance standards and oversight. These measures included stricter requirements for maintenance documentation, improved training programs for maintenance personnel, and increased emphasis on quality control and safety management systems.

The tragedy of AeroPerú Flight 603 serves as a stark reminder of the interconnectedness of various elements within the aviation system and the need for constant vigilance in all aspects of aircraft operation and maintenance. The loss of 70 lives due to a preventable error highlights the critical importance of adherence to procedures, thorough training, and effective oversight in ensuring the safety of air travel.

Memorials and tributes were established to honor the victims of Flight 603, and efforts were made to support their families and provide them with the necessary resources to cope with their loss. The aviation community mourned the tragedy but also used it as a catalyst for positive change, reinforcing the commitment to safety and the continuous improvement of aviation standards.

The legacy of AeroPerú Flight 603 endures as a poignant lesson in the importance of meticulous maintenance practices and the relentless pursuit of safety in aviation. The lessons learned from this disaster have contributed to the development of more robust maintenance protocols and oversight mechanisms, helping to prevent similar tragedies in the future. The memory of those who lost their lives on Flight 603 continues to inspire the aviation community to uphold the highest standards of safety and professionalism in all aspects of air travel.

Chapter 28: Spanair Flight 5022

Spanair Flight 5022 was a scheduled domestic passenger flight from Madrid-Barajas Airport in Madrid, Spain, to Gran Canaria Airport in the Canary Islands. On August 20, 2008, the McDonnell Douglas MD-82 aircraft operating the flight crashed during takeoff, resulting in the deaths of 154 people and injuries to 18 others. This tragic accident remains one of Spain's deadliest aviation disasters and prompted a detailed investigation into the causes, revealing significant issues related to aircraft maintenance, pilot training, and safety procedures.

The aircraft involved in the accident was a McDonnell Douglas MD-82, registered as EC-HFP, which had been in service since 1993. On the day of the accident, the flight was under the command of Captain Antonio García Luna and First Officer Francisco Javier Mulet Bayona. Captain Luna had accumulated approximately 8,475 flight hours, with 1,235 hours on the MD-80 series, while First Officer Mulet had around 2,700 flight hours, with 1,174 hours on the MD-80 series. There were 166 passengers and six crew members on board.

On the morning of August 20, Flight 5022 was scheduled to depart from Madrid-Barajas Airport at 1:00 PM local time. However, the flight was delayed due to a technical issue with the aircraft's ram air temperature (RAT) probe, which measures air temperature for the air conditioning system. The problem was reported and addressed by maintenance personnel, who deactivated the probe heater, considering it non-essential for the flight. The aircraft was cleared for departure, and the flight crew prepared for takeoff.

At 2:23 PM, Flight 5022 taxied to Runway 36L for takeoff. The takeoff roll commenced, and the aircraft accelerated down the runway. However, shortly after liftoff, the aircraft began to experience difficulties. The plane failed to gain sufficient altitude and began to lose airspeed. Witnesses reported seeing the aircraft veer to the right and then back to the left before crashing into a ravine near the runway, approximately 1,000 meters from the runway's end.

The impact caused the aircraft to break apart and catch fire, leading to a catastrophic scene. Emergency response teams were quickly dispatched to the crash site, but the intensity of the fire and the scattered wreckage complicated rescue efforts. Out of the 172 people on board, only 18 survived, suffering various degrees of injuries. The majority of the passengers and crew perished in the crash, making it one of the deadliest aviation accidents in Spain's history.

The immediate aftermath of the crash saw a massive mobilization of emergency services, including firefighters, medical personnel, and law enforcement. The survivors were transported to nearby hospitals for treatment, while authorities worked to recover the bodies of the deceased and secure the crash site. The Spanish Civil Aviation Accident and Incident Investigation Commission (CIAIAC) initiated a thorough investigation to determine the cause of the accident, with assistance from international experts, including the U.S. National Transportation Safety Board (NTSB) and the aircraft's manufacturer, Boeing (which had acquired McDonnell Douglas).

The investigation focused on several key areas, including the aircraft's maintenance history, the actions of the flight crew, and the performance of the aircraft's systems. One of the critical pieces of evidence was the flight data recorder (FDR) and cockpit voice recorder (CVR), which were recovered from the wreckage. Analysis of the data from these recorders provided crucial insights into the sequence of events leading up to the crash.

One of the primary findings of the investigation was that the aircraft's flaps and slats were not extended for takeoff. These devices are essential for generating the necessary lift during takeoff, and their improper configuration significantly contributed to the aircraft's inability to gain altitude. The investigation revealed that the flight crew had failed to deploy the flaps and slats as required for takeoff.

The absence of the takeoff configuration warning system (TOWS) alarm, which should have alerted the flight crew to the incorrect configuration, was another critical factor. The TOWS system is designed to provide an audible warning if the aircraft is not configured correctly for takeoff. However, the system did not activate during the takeoff roll of Flight 5022. The investigation determined that the failure of the TOWS alarm was linked to the deactivation of the RAT probe heater, which had been carried out as part of the earlier maintenance actions. This deactivation inadvertently disabled the TOWS system, preventing it from issuing the necessary warning.

Further analysis of the cockpit voice recorder revealed that the flight crew had not completed the takeoff checklist properly. The checklist includes critical steps to ensure that the aircraft is correctly configured for takeoff, including the deployment of flaps and slats. The investigation found that the flight crew's attention may have been distracted by various factors, including the earlier technical issue and the subsequent delay, leading to the oversight.

The investigation also highlighted deficiencies in Spanair's maintenance practices and safety culture. The airline's procedures for addressing technical issues and ensuring proper configuration of aircraft systems were found to be inadequate. The oversight in maintenance, particularly the impact of deactivating the RAT probe heater on the TOWS system, demonstrated a lack of comprehensive risk assessment and coordination between maintenance and flight operations.

The CIAIAC's final report, released in 2011, identified multiple contributing factors to the crash of Flight 5022. These included the failure to extend the flaps and slats, the malfunction of the TOWS system, the inadequate maintenance procedures, and the flight crew's failure to properly complete the takeoff checklist. The report made several recommendations aimed at improving safety practices within Spanair and across the aviation industry.

One of the key recommendations was for airlines to enhance their maintenance procedures to ensure that any changes or deactivations of aircraft systems are thoroughly assessed for potential safety implications. The report also emphasized the importance of rigorous adherence to checklists by flight crews and the need for continuous training to reinforce the criticality of these procedures. Additionally, the report called for improvements in the design and reliability of warning systems like TOWS to prevent similar failures in the future.

The crash of Spanair Flight 5022 had significant repercussions for the airline and the broader aviation community. Spanair faced intense scrutiny and criticism for its safety practices, leading to a decline in passenger confidence and financial difficulties. In 2012, less than four years after the accident, Spanair ceased operations and filed for bankruptcy.

The impact of the crash extended beyond Spanair, prompting a review of safety practices and regulatory oversight across the aviation industry. Authorities in Spain and other countries implemented changes to enhance the safety of flight operations, maintenance procedures, and pilot training. The accident underscored the importance of a robust safety culture, meticulous adherence to procedures, and effective communication between maintenance and flight operations.

For the families of the victims, the crash of Flight 5022 was a devastating and life-altering event. The loss of loved ones and the traumatic nature of the accident left deep emotional scars. Memorial services and commemorations were held to honor the victims, and support organizations were established to provide assistance to the affected families. In Madrid, a memorial garden was created near the crash site, featuring a sculpture and plaques bearing the names of the victims, serving as a place of reflection and remembrance.

The legal aftermath of the crash included lawsuits filed by the victims' families against Spanair and other parties, seeking compensation for their losses. The legal proceedings highlighted the complex interplay of responsibilities among airlines, maintenance providers, and regulatory authorities in ensuring aviation safety. The settlements and compensations provided some measure of justice for the families, but the emotional and psychological impact of the tragedy continued to resonate.

In the broader context of aviation safety, the crash of Spanair Flight 5022 served as a stark reminder of the critical importance of rigorous maintenance practices, thorough training, and adherence to procedures. The lessons learned from the investigation have been integrated into safety protocols and training programs across the industry, contributing to the ongoing efforts to enhance the safety of air travel.

The legacy of Flight 5022 is reflected in the improvements made to aviation safety as a result of the lessons learned from the accident. The tragedy underscored the need for continuous vigilance, the importance of addressing technical issues comprehensively, and the necessity of fostering a safety-first culture within the aviation industry. While the memory of those who perished in the crash remains a source of sorrow, their legacy continues to drive efforts to prevent similar accidents and ensure the highest standards of safety in aviation.

Chapter 29: Iran Air Flight 655

Iran Air Flight 655 was a scheduled passenger flight from Tehran, Iran, to Dubai, United Arab Emirates, with a stopover in Bandar Abbas, Iran. On July 3, 1988, the flight was shot down by the USS Vincennes, a United States Navy guided missile cruiser, over the Persian Gulf. All 290 people on board were killed, making it one of the deadliest air disasters in history. The incident occurred during the Iran-Iraq War and led to a significant diplomatic crisis between Iran and the United States. It remains a deeply controversial and tragic event, raising critical questions about military engagement, rules of engagement, and the protection of civilian lives during armed conflict.

The aircraft involved was an Airbus A300B2-203, registered as EP-IBU. It was operated by Iran Air, the national airline of Iran. On that fateful day, Flight 655 took off from Tehran Mehrabad International Airport at approximately 10:17 AM local time and landed in Bandar Abbas at 11:02 AM for a scheduled stopover. The aircraft departed from Bandar Abbas at 10:47 AM UTC (14:17 local time) and began its ascent to its cruising altitude of 14,000 feet. The flight plan for Flight 655 was filed and adhered to civilian air traffic control procedures, and the aircraft was equipped with standard identification and communication systems.

The USS Vincennes (CG-49) was patrolling the Persian Gulf at the time of the incident. The vessel was equipped with the Aegis Combat System, an advanced radar and missile guidance system designed to track and engage multiple targets simultaneously. The Vincennes, commanded by Captain William C. Rogers III, was involved in a skirmish with Iranian gunboats in the Strait of Hormuz shortly before the incident. Tensions in the region were high, as the Iran-Iraq War had led to increased military activity and the targeting of commercial shipping by both belligerent states.

As Flight 655 departed Bandar Abbas, it climbed to an altitude of 12,000 feet. At the same time, the USS Vincennes, which was engaged in a surface battle with Iranian gunboats, detected an aircraft ascending from Bandar Abbas. The crew of the Vincennes misidentified the ascending Airbus A300 as an Iranian F-14 Tomcat, a fighter jet known to be operated by the Iranian Air Force. The radar operators on the Vincennes reported that the aircraft was descending and accelerating towards the cruiser, interpreting this as a hostile maneuver.

Despite multiple attempts to establish contact with the aircraft on both military and civilian communication frequencies, there was no response from the flight crew of Flight 655. However, the aircraft was on a routine civilian flight path and squawking the correct transponder code for a commercial flight. The flight crew, busy with the routine tasks of operating the aircraft, may not have been monitoring the military frequencies used by the Vincennes.

The misidentification of Flight 655 as a hostile aircraft led Captain Rogers to authorize the launch of two SM-2MR surface-to-air missiles at 10:54 AM UTC (14:24 local time). The missiles struck the Airbus A300, causing it to disintegrate in mid-air. The wreckage fell into the Persian Gulf, and all 290 people on board, including 66 children and 16 crew members, perished in the explosion and subsequent crash. The majority of the passengers were Iranian nationals, but there were also citizens from Italy, India, Pakistan, and the UAE among the victims.

The immediate aftermath of the shootdown was characterized by confusion and shock. The United States initially defended the actions of the Vincennes, stating that the crew had acted in self-defense and in accordance with the rules of engagement. President Ronald Reagan expressed deep regret over the loss of life but maintained that the incident was a tragic mistake. Iran, on the other hand, vehemently condemned the shootdown as a deliberate and barbaric act, demanding international condemnation and reparations.

Investigations into the incident were conducted by both the United States and international bodies. The U.S. Navy conducted an internal investigation, which concluded that the crew of the Vincennes had acted within the bounds of their training and the information available to them at the time. However, the investigation also highlighted several critical errors in judgment and procedure. The misidentification of the Airbus A300 as an F-14 Tomcat was a key factor, as was the failure to properly assess the flight profile and transponder signals of the aircraft.

The International Civil Aviation Organization (ICAO) also conducted an investigation, which was more critical of the actions of the Vincennes' crew. The ICAO report noted that the flight path of Iran Air Flight 655 was consistent with a commercial airliner and that the aircraft was operating in a recognized civilian air corridor. The report criticized the failure to use all available means to positively identify the aircraft before engaging and questioned the adequacy of the rules of engagement and communication protocols in place.

The legal and diplomatic fallout from the incident was significant. Iran brought a case against the United States in the International Court of Justice (ICJ), alleging that the shootdown violated international law. The case, Iran v. United States, focused on the principles of sovereignty, the protection of civilian lives, and the conduct of military operations in international airspace. In 1996, the United States and Iran reached a settlement agreement, which included an expression of deep regret by the U.S. government and the payment of $61.8 million in compensation to the families of the victims. However, the settlement did not include an explicit admission of legal liability by the United States.

The shootdown of Iran Air Flight 655 had far-reaching implications for international aviation safety and military engagement protocols. One of the key lessons learned from the incident was the importance of clear communication and identification procedures to prevent similar tragedies. The ICAO and other aviation authorities implemented changes to improve the safety of civilian airliners operating in conflict zones, including better coordination between military and civilian air traffic control and enhanced training for aircrew and military personnel on the identification of civilian aircraft.

The incident also prompted a reevaluation of the rules of engagement for military forces operating in complex and high-tension environments. The need for stringent verification procedures before engaging potential threats was emphasized, and changes were made to ensure that military personnel had better situational awareness and access to comprehensive intelligence before making critical decisions.

For the families of the victims, the shootdown of Flight 655 was a devastating loss that left a lasting impact. Memorials and commemorations were held in Iran and other countries to honor the memory of those who perished. The emotional and psychological toll on the families was profound, as they grappled with the sudden and tragic loss of their loved ones. Support organizations and advocacy groups emerged to provide assistance and to ensure that the voices of the victims' families were heard in the pursuit of justice and accountability.

In the broader context of U.S.-Iran relations, the incident further strained an already tense relationship. The Iran-Iraq War had created a volatile environment in the Persian Gulf, and the shootdown of Flight 655 exacerbated the animosity between the two nations. The incident remains a point of contention in the historical narrative of U.S.-Iran relations, symbolizing the broader geopolitical and military tensions that have characterized the relationship for decades.

The legacy of Iran Air Flight 655 is a sobering reminder of the tragic consequences that can arise from miscommunication, misidentification, and the complexities of military operations in conflict zones. The incident underscored the necessity of robust safety protocols, rigorous training, and the prioritization of civilian lives in military engagements. It also highlighted the importance of international cooperation and the development of comprehensive frameworks to ensure the safety of air travel in regions of conflict.

Over the years, efforts to improve aviation safety and military engagement protocols have continued, informed by the lessons learned from Flight 655 and other similar tragedies. The aviation industry and military forces have worked to enhance their communication systems, identification procedures, and rules of engagement to prevent the recurrence of such incidents. The commitment to these improvements reflects a collective determination to honor the memory of those who lost their lives and to ensure that the skies remain safe for all who travel.

Chapter 30: Turkish Airlines Flight 981

Turkish Airlines Flight 981 was a scheduled international passenger flight from Istanbul Atatürk Airport in Turkey to London Heathrow Airport in the United Kingdom, with an intermediate stop at Orly Airport in Paris, France. On March 3, 1974, the McDonnell Douglas DC-10 aircraft operating the flight crashed into the Ermenonville Forest near Paris, resulting in the deaths of all 346 passengers and crew on board. This disaster, known as the Ermenonville air disaster, was one of the deadliest aviation accidents in history at the time and highlighted critical issues in aircraft design, maintenance, and safety procedures.

The aircraft involved in the accident was a McDonnell Douglas DC-10-10, registered as TC-JAV and named "Ankara." It had been delivered to Turkish Airlines in December 1972. The DC-10 was a wide-body airliner designed for long-haul flights and was equipped with advanced features for its time. However, the aircraft's design included a critical flaw in the cargo door mechanism, which played a significant role in the disaster.

On the morning of March 3, 1974, Turkish Airlines Flight 981 departed from Istanbul Atatürk Airport at approximately 07:57 UTC (09:57 local time) bound for Orly Airport in Paris. The flight was under the command of Captain Nejat Berköz, a highly experienced pilot with over 7,000 flight hours, and First Officer Oral Ulusman, who had accumulated around 5,600 flight hours. The flight was carrying a full load of passengers, including many British citizens who had transferred from an earlier, overbooked British European Airways flight.

The first leg of the flight from Istanbul to Paris proceeded uneventfully, and the aircraft landed at Orly Airport at around 11:02 UTC. After a brief stopover, during which passengers disembarked and new passengers boarded, Flight 981 was prepared for the final leg of its journey to London Heathrow. The aircraft was refueled, and baggage and cargo were loaded into the lower holds. Among the cargo was a substantial load of baggage, reflecting the high number of passengers on board.

At 12:32 UTC, Flight 981 took off from Orly Airport and began its climb to cruising altitude. The flight path took the aircraft over the Ermenonville Forest, northeast of Paris. Approximately 10 minutes after takeoff, at an altitude of around 12,000 feet, the cargo door in the rear fuselage suddenly burst open. The explosive decompression caused a rapid and catastrophic chain of events. The force of the decompression caused the cabin floor above the cargo hold to collapse, severing control cables to the aircraft's tail surfaces and two of its engines. As a result, the pilots lost control of the aircraft.

The flight crew's efforts to regain control of the DC-10 were in vain. The aircraft entered a steep descent, rapidly losing altitude. At 12:40 UTC, just eight minutes after the decompression, the DC-10 crashed into the Ermenonville Forest at high speed. The impact was devastating, and the aircraft was completely destroyed. There were no survivors among the 346 passengers and crew on board.

The crash site in the Ermenonville Forest was a scene of widespread devastation, with wreckage scattered over a wide area. Emergency response teams were quickly dispatched to the site, but the severity of the impact and the extent of the destruction meant that there was little they could do. Recovery efforts focused on retrieving the bodies of the victims and gathering evidence to determine the cause of the disaster.

The investigation into the crash of Turkish Airlines Flight 981 was led by the French Bureau d'Enquêtes et d'Analyses pour la sécurité de l'aviation civile (BEA), with assistance from international experts, including representatives from McDonnell Douglas and the U.S. National Transportation Safety Board (NTSB). The investigation team faced the challenging task of piecing together the events leading up to the crash from the wreckage and the flight data recorders.

One of the critical pieces of evidence recovered from the crash site was the aircraft's cargo door. The investigation revealed that the cargo door had suffered a catastrophic failure, leading to the explosive decompression. The DC-10's cargo door was a unique design, featuring an outward-opening mechanism. This design allowed for more cargo space but also required a complex locking mechanism to ensure the door's integrity during flight.

The investigation found that the cargo door's locking mechanism had not engaged properly. Specifically, the door's latches had not fully rotated into the locked position, even though the handle indicated that the door was secure. This discrepancy was due to a design flaw that allowed the door to appear locked even when the latches were not fully engaged. During the flight, the pressure differential between the cabin and the outside air caused the improperly locked door to burst open, leading to the explosive decompression.

Further analysis revealed that the issue with the cargo door was not new. There had been previous incidents involving the DC-10's cargo door, including a near-disaster involving American Airlines Flight 96 in 1972. In that incident, the cargo door had also failed, leading to a loss of cabin pressure. However, the crew managed to land the aircraft safely, and the incident prompted an investigation by the NTSB. The investigation had identified the design flaw in the cargo door and issued recommendations for modifications to enhance its safety.

Despite the recommendations, McDonnell Douglas had implemented only partial modifications to the cargo door design. The modifications included a viewing port for ground crew to verify the engagement of the door latches, but the fundamental design flaw remained unaddressed. The failure to fully implement the necessary modifications and address the underlying issue contributed directly to the disaster of Flight 981.

The BEA's final report, released in 1976, identified the cargo door failure as the primary cause of the accident. The report criticized

McDonnell Douglas for not taking adequate measures to rectify the known design flaw and for not ensuring that the modifications were properly implemented across the DC-10 fleet. The report also highlighted deficiencies in the maintenance and inspection procedures used by Turkish Airlines and the ground handling crew at Orly Airport.

The crash of Turkish Airlines Flight 981 had profound implications for the aviation industry. The disaster exposed serious shortcomings in aircraft design, certification, and regulatory oversight. In response to the findings, McDonnell Douglas implemented comprehensive redesigns of the DC-10's cargo door mechanism to ensure that such a failure could not occur again. These changes included the addition of vents to equalize pressure, reinforced locking mechanisms, and improved indicators for the proper engagement of door latches.

The incident also led to significant changes in aviation regulations and safety practices. The Federal Aviation Administration (FAA) and other regulatory bodies around the world introduced stricter certification standards for aircraft doors and emergency procedures for handling decompression events. Airlines were required to implement more rigorous inspection and maintenance protocols to ensure the safety of their fleets.

The impact of the disaster on Turkish Airlines was severe. The airline faced intense scrutiny and criticism for its maintenance practices and the oversight of its fleet. The loss of 346 lives, including many British citizens, had a lasting emotional and psychological impact on the victims' families and the broader public. Memorial services and commemorations were held in honor of the victims, and support organizations were established to provide assistance to the affected families.

In the broader context of aviation history, the crash of Turkish Airlines Flight 981 remains a stark reminder of the importance of rigorous safety standards, meticulous maintenance practices, and the continuous improvement of aircraft design. The lessons learned from the disaster have informed safety protocols and regulatory frameworks that continue to evolve in the pursuit of safer air travel.

In addition to the technical and regulatory changes prompted by the crash, the disaster also had a lasting influence on the culture of aviation safety. The emphasis on proactive identification and resolution of potential design flaws, thorough testing and certification processes, and the importance of clear and effective communication among manufacturers, regulators, and airlines became central to the industry's approach to safety.

The legacy of Turkish Airlines Flight 981 extends beyond the immediate aftermath of the disaster. It serves as a case study in the critical importance of addressing known issues comprehensively and the dangers of complacency in the face of safety concerns. The improvements in aircraft design and safety regulations that followed the crash have contributed to a significant reduction in the frequency and severity of aviation accidents in subsequent decades.

The memorialization of the victims of Flight 981 continues to be an important aspect of the disaster's legacy. Monuments and memorials have been erected to honor the memory of those who lost their lives, providing a place of reflection and remembrance for their families and the public. The ongoing support for the victims' families underscores the enduring impact of the disaster and the importance of community and compassion in the wake of tragedy.

Chapter 31: United Airlines Flight 232

United Airlines Flight 232 was a scheduled passenger flight from Denver, Colorado, to Chicago, Illinois, with a final destination of Philadelphia, Pennsylvania. On July 19, 1989, the flight experienced a catastrophic failure of its tail-mounted engine, leading to the loss of all hydraulic control systems. Despite the extreme difficulties faced by the flight crew, they managed to execute an emergency landing at Sioux Gateway Airport in Sioux City, Iowa. Of the 296 people on board, 111 lost their lives, but the remarkable efforts of the crew and rescuers saved 185 lives. The incident is widely studied in aviation for its lessons on emergency response, crew resource management, and aircraft design.

The aircraft involved was a McDonnell Douglas DC-10-10, registered as N1819U. The DC-10 is a wide-body, three-engine jet airliner, with one engine mounted on each wing and a third engine mounted at the base of the vertical stabilizer at the tail. United Airlines Flight 232 departed Denver's Stapleton International Airport at 2:09 PM MDT with 285 passengers and 11 crew members on board. The flight was under the command of Captain Alfred C. Haynes, First Officer William R. Records, and Second Officer Dudley J. Dvorak. Captain Haynes was an experienced pilot with over 29,000 flight hours, and both Records and Dvorak were also seasoned aviators.

At approximately 3:16 PM CDT, while cruising at 37,000 feet over western Iowa, the aircraft suffered an uncontained failure of its tail-mounted General Electric CF6-6D engine. The failure caused debris to be ejected at high velocity, severing the lines of all three of the aircraft's hydraulic systems. Hydraulic fluid is essential for the operation of an aircraft's control surfaces, including the ailerons, rudder, and elevators. The loss of hydraulic pressure meant that the flight crew lost all conventional means of controlling the aircraft.

Despite the dire situation, Captain Haynes and his crew remained calm and began to assess their options. They quickly realized that they could not control the aircraft using the standard flight controls. Instead, they discovered that by adjusting the thrust of the remaining two engines, they could achieve a modicum of control over the aircraft's direction and altitude. This form of control, known as "differential thrust," involved increasing or decreasing power to the engines to induce roll and pitch changes. This method was highly unconventional and had never been used to land a commercial airliner under such conditions.

Meanwhile, United Airlines Flight 232 declared an emergency and requested vectors to the nearest suitable airport. Air traffic controllers directed the aircraft toward Sioux Gateway Airport in Sioux City, Iowa, which had a long runway suitable for an emergency landing. Captain Haynes and his crew informed the passengers of the situation, advising them to prepare for a crash landing. Flight attendants worked to secure the cabin and instruct passengers on the brace position to minimize injuries upon impact.

As Flight 232 approached Sioux City, Captain Haynes was joined by Captain Dennis E. Fitch, a United Airlines DC-10 flight instructor who was traveling as a passenger. Fitch offered his assistance, and together with the flight crew, they continued to use differential thrust to steer the aircraft. Their combined efforts resulted in a controlled, albeit erratic, descent toward the airport. The situation was further complicated by the fact that the aircraft's speed was difficult to control, and it was descending at a faster rate than ideal.

At 4:00 PM CDT, Flight 232 began its final approach to Runway 22 at Sioux Gateway Airport. The approach was unstable, with the aircraft oscillating from side to side and losing altitude rapidly. Despite their best efforts, the crew could not maintain a proper glide slope. As the aircraft neared the runway, it veered to the right, causing the right wing to dip and strike the ground first. The impact caused the aircraft to break apart, with the fuselage cartwheeling down the runway and into a nearby cornfield. The crash resulted in a massive fireball as fuel ignited upon impact.

Emergency response teams at Sioux Gateway Airport were well-prepared, having conducted a disaster drill just weeks before. Firefighters, paramedics, and other emergency personnel rushed to the scene to assist survivors and extinguish the fires. The coordinated and rapid response of the emergency teams was crucial in saving many lives. Remarkably, 185 of the 296 people on board survived the crash, including Captain Haynes and the other members of the flight crew.

The National Transportation Safety Board (NTSB) launched a comprehensive investigation into the crash of United Airlines Flight 232. The investigation revealed that the uncontained failure of the number two (tail-mounted) engine was caused by a fatigue crack in a titanium alloy fan disk. The crack had gone undetected during routine maintenance inspections, highlighting a critical vulnerability in the inspection process for engine components. The NTSB's final report, released in 1990, identified the failure of the fan disk as the probable cause of the accident and emphasized the need for improved inspection techniques and materials testing to prevent similar failures in the future.

The loss of all three hydraulic systems was another focus of the investigation. The DC-10's design relied on redundant hydraulic systems to provide backup control in case of a single system failure. However, the placement of the hydraulic lines in close proximity to the engines meant that an uncontained engine failure could sever all the lines simultaneously. The NTSB recommended design changes to improve the separation and protection of hydraulic lines, as well as the development of alternative systems to provide control in the event of a complete hydraulic failure.

The crash of United Airlines Flight 232 had a profound impact on the aviation industry. McDonnell Douglas, the manufacturer of the DC-10, and General Electric, the engine manufacturer, implemented significant changes to their designs and maintenance procedures based on the findings of the investigation. The Federal Aviation Administration (FAA) introduced new regulations requiring more rigorous inspection and testing of critical engine components. The industry also adopted improved materials and manufacturing processes to enhance the durability and reliability of engine parts.

One of the most significant outcomes of the Flight 232 crash was the increased emphasis on crew resource management (CRM) in pilot training. CRM focuses on effective communication, teamwork, and decision-making among flight crew members to handle emergencies and complex situations. The collaboration between Captain Haynes, First Officer Records, Second Officer Dvorak, and Captain Fitch during the Flight 232 emergency became a textbook example of successful CRM. Their ability to work together under extreme stress and utilize each other's expertise was instrumental in saving many lives.

The heroism and professionalism displayed by the crew of Flight 232 were widely recognized and celebrated. Captain Haynes and his crew received numerous awards and honors for their actions, including the United States Airline Pilots Association's Gold Medal for heroism. The crew's handling of the emergency became a case study in aviation safety and CRM training programs worldwide.

The survivors of Flight 232 and the families of the victims formed a close-knit community in the aftermath of the crash. Support groups and memorials were established to honor the memory of those who perished and to provide assistance to the survivors. The annual reunions and commemorative events held in Sioux City serve as a testament to the resilience and strength of the survivors and their families. The crash site at Sioux Gateway Airport features a memorial sculpture, "The Spirit of Siouxland," dedicated to the victims and the heroes of Flight 232.

In the years following the crash, advancements in aircraft design and safety systems continued to build on the lessons learned from

Flight 232. Modern aircraft are equipped with enhanced redundancy and fail-safe mechanisms to prevent the loss of control in the event of a hydraulic failure. The development of fly-by-wire technology, which replaces traditional hydraulic controls with electronic systems, has further improved the safety and reliability of commercial airliners.

The legacy of United Airlines Flight 232 extends beyond the immediate changes in regulations and technology. The incident highlighted the critical importance of thorough maintenance and inspection practices, the need for continuous improvement in aircraft design, and the value of effective teamwork and communication in emergency situations. The story of Flight 232 serves as a powerful reminder of the human capacity for courage, ingenuity, and resilience in the face of adversity.

For aviation professionals and enthusiasts, the crash of Flight 232 is a profound and enduring lesson in the complexities of flight safety. It underscores the necessity of vigilance, continuous learning, and the relentless pursuit of excellence in all aspects of aviation. The improvements in safety that followed the disaster have contributed to the ongoing efforts to make air travel one of the safest modes of transportation in the world.

Chapter 32: Colgan Air Flight 3407

Colgan Air Flight 3407, operating as Continental Connection Flight 3407, was a scheduled passenger flight from Newark Liberty International Airport in Newark, New Jersey, to Buffalo Niagara International Airport in Buffalo, New York. On the night of February 12, 2009, the flight crashed into a residential neighborhood in Clarence Center, New York, approximately five miles from its destination, killing all 49 people on board and one person on the ground. The crash, one of the deadliest in recent U.S. aviation history, brought to light significant issues in the regional airline industry, including pilot training, fatigue, and safety regulations.

The aircraft involved in the accident was a Bombardier Dash 8 Q400, a twin-engine turboprop regional airliner, operated by Colgan Air on behalf of Continental Airlines. The plane, tail number N200WQ, was nearly a year old and had logged approximately 2,247 flight hours. The flight crew consisted of Captain Marvin Renslow, First Officer Rebecca Shaw, and two flight attendants. Captain Renslow, aged 47, had accumulated 3,379 flight hours, including 111 hours on the Q400, while First Officer Shaw, aged 24, had logged 2,244 flight hours, with 774 hours on the Q400.

The flight departed Newark at 9:18 PM EST and was scheduled to land in Buffalo at 10:17 PM. The weather conditions in Buffalo that night included light snow, mist, and icing conditions, common for the region during winter. As the aircraft approached Buffalo, it was placed in a holding pattern due to air traffic congestion. At approximately 10:05 PM, air traffic control cleared Flight 3407 to descend and proceed with the approach to Runway 23.

During the descent, the flight crew encountered icing conditions, which they reported to air traffic control. Icing can affect an aircraft's performance by disrupting airflow over the wings and increasing weight. The Q400 is equipped with de-icing systems, including pneumatic boots on the wings and tail surfaces, designed to break up ice accumulation. The crew activated these systems as they prepared for the approach.

At 10:12 PM, as the aircraft was descending through 2,300 feet at a speed of 185 knots, the autopilot disconnected, and the aircraft abruptly pitched up. The stick shaker, a device that vibrates the control column to warn pilots of an impending stall, activated. Despite these warnings, Captain Renslow pulled back on the control column, raising the nose of the aircraft, which exacerbated the situation. The proper recovery technique for a stall is to lower the nose to regain airspeed and lift.

The aircraft's speed continued to decrease, and it entered an aerodynamic stall. As the plane pitched up further, it rolled to the left and then to the right, entering a steep descent. The flight data recorder (FDR) and cockpit voice recorder (CVR) captured the frantic attempts by the crew to regain control, but their efforts were unsuccessful. At 10:17 PM, Flight 3407 crashed into a house in Clarence Center, erupting into flames upon impact. The impact and ensuing fire killed all 49 people on board and a 61-year-old resident in the house, Doug Wielinski, who was the only person at home at the time.

The National Transportation Safety Board (NTSB) launched an immediate investigation into the crash. The investigation team included representatives from the Federal Aviation Administration (FAA), Colgan Air, Bombardier (the aircraft manufacturer), and other relevant parties. The NTSB focused on several key areas: the aircraft's performance, the flight crew's actions, and the environmental conditions.

The examination of the wreckage revealed that the aircraft's de-icing systems were functioning correctly, and the engines were producing power up to the moment of impact. This eliminated mechanical failure and pointed to human factors as a primary cause.

The NTSB's analysis of the FDR and CVR data indicated that the flight crew's response to the stall warning was inappropriate and directly contributed to the loss of control.

The NTSB's investigation highlighted several critical issues related to pilot training and performance. Captain Renslow had failed multiple proficiency checks during his career but had been retrained and allowed to continue flying. First Officer Shaw had limited experience flying in icy conditions and had spent the previous night commuting from Seattle, Washington, to Newark, resulting in potential fatigue.

Fatigue emerged as a significant factor in the crash. Both pilots had spent a long time commuting before starting their duty period. Captain Renslow had traveled from Florida, and First Officer Shaw from Seattle. By the time they began the flight, both were likely experiencing significant fatigue, which can impair cognitive and motor skills. Fatigue can also affect decision-making, situational awareness, and reaction times, all of which are critical in an emergency.

The NTSB's investigation revealed that Colgan Air's training programs did not adequately address stall recovery techniques. The training focused on preventing stalls rather than recovering from them, which left pilots unprepared to handle an actual stall scenario. The investigation also identified deficiencies in Colgan Air's procedures for assessing pilot proficiency and ensuring that pilots adhered to proper rest and duty time regulations.

Another crucial finding was the flight crew's failure to properly manage the aircraft's airspeed during the approach. The crew allowed the speed to decrease to a dangerously low level, triggering the stall warning. Properly managing airspeed, especially in icing conditions, is vital to maintaining safe flight. The NTSB noted that the crew did not adhere to standard operating procedures, which require maintaining a minimum airspeed in such conditions.

The NTSB's final report, released in 2010, identified the probable cause of the accident as the captain's inappropriate response to the activation of the stick shaker, which led to an aerodynamic stall from which the airplane did not recover. Contributing factors included the flight crew's failure to monitor airspeed, the captain's failure to manage the flight effectively, Colgan Air's inadequate training program, and the FAA's insufficient oversight of Colgan Air's operations.

The crash of Colgan Air Flight 3407 had a profound impact on the aviation industry and regulatory environment. The tragedy underscored the need for more stringent regulations regarding pilot training, fatigue management, and airline oversight. In response to the accident, the FAA implemented several significant changes aimed at improving safety in the regional airline industry.

One of the most notable changes was the implementation of new pilot training requirements. The FAA mandated that all pilots must complete additional training in stall recognition and recovery, upset recovery, and other critical skills. The new regulations also required pilots to undergo more comprehensive initial and recurrent training programs to ensure proficiency in handling emergencies.

The FAA also addressed the issue of pilot fatigue by revising the regulations governing flight and duty time limitations. The new rules, which took effect in 2014, set stricter limits on the number of hours pilots can work and mandated minimum rest periods between duty periods. These regulations aimed to reduce fatigue-related errors and improve overall safety in the aviation industry.

Another significant change was the introduction of the Airline Safety and Federal Aviation Administration Extension Act of 2010, commonly known as the "Pilot Bill of Rights." This legislation raised the minimum flight experience required for first officers on commercial airlines to 1,500 hours, the same as captains. The act also mandated the establishment of a database to track pilots' training records and performance history, ensuring that airlines have access to comprehensive information when hiring new pilots.

The crash of Flight 3407 also led to increased scrutiny of regional airlines and their relationships with major carriers. Regional airlines, which often operate flights under the branding of major airlines, were found to have varying levels of safety standards and practices. The FAA and other regulatory bodies took steps to ensure that regional airlines adhere to the same high standards as their larger counterparts.

The families of the victims of Flight 3407 played a crucial role in advocating for these changes. They formed the group "Families of Continental Flight 3407" and tirelessly campaigned for improved safety regulations. Their efforts brought national attention to the issues of pilot training, fatigue, and airline oversight, ultimately leading to significant reforms in the industry.

The legacy of Colgan Air Flight 3407 continues to influence aviation safety today. The crash serves as a sobering reminder of the importance of rigorous training, proper fatigue management, and strict adherence to safety procedures. The changes implemented in the wake of the tragedy have contributed to a safer aviation environment and have helped prevent similar accidents from occurring.

Chapter 33: PSA Flight 182

Pacific Southwest Airlines (PSA) Flight 182 was a scheduled passenger flight from Sacramento, California, to San Diego, California, with an intermediate stop in Los Angeles. On September 25, 1978, the flight tragically ended in a mid-air collision with a private Cessna 172 aircraft over San Diego. The collision caused both planes to crash into the North Park neighborhood, resulting in the deaths of all 135 people on board the PSA aircraft, the two occupants of the Cessna, and seven people on the ground. The disaster remains one of the deadliest aviation accidents in U.S. history and had profound implications for aviation safety and air traffic control procedures.

The aircraft involved in the accident was a Boeing 727-214, a popular tri-jet airliner, registered as N533PS. On the morning of the accident, PSA Flight 182 departed from Sacramento at 8:16 AM PDT, bound for San Diego via Los Angeles. The flight was under the command of Captain James McFeron, First Officer Robert Fox, and Flight Engineer Martin Wahne. Captain McFeron was an experienced pilot with over 14,000 flight hours, and both First Officer Fox and Flight Engineer Wahne were also seasoned aviators.

The private aircraft involved was a Cessna 172, registered as N7711G, operated by student pilot David Boswell and his instructor, Martin Kazy. The Cessna was conducting a training flight in the San Diego area. The airspace around San Diego's Lindbergh Field, now known as San Diego International Airport, was particularly busy, with numerous private and commercial flights converging on the region.

At approximately 8:59 AM, PSA Flight 182 was descending towards Lindbergh Field, preparing for an approach to Runway 27. At the same time, the Cessna 172 was performing practice instrument landings at the nearby Montgomery Field, a smaller airport located to the northeast of Lindbergh Field. Both aircraft were under the control of the San Diego Terminal Radar Approach Control (TRACON), which was responsible for managing the dense air traffic in the area.

As Flight 182 approached San Diego, the crew was informed by TRACON that they had traffic at 12 o'clock, one mile away, and slightly below them, which was the Cessna 172. The PSA crew acknowledged the traffic advisory and reported having the Cessna in sight. The PSA flight was then cleared to continue its descent and maintain visual separation from the Cessna. However, a critical miscommunication occurred: the PSA crew misidentified a different aircraft as the Cessna and thus believed they had safely passed the Cessna.

At 9:01 AM, the two aircraft collided at an altitude of about 2,600 feet. The right wing of the Boeing 727 struck the Cessna, causing catastrophic damage to both planes. The Cessna was immediately rendered uncontrollable and broke apart, while the right wing of the 727 was heavily damaged, leading to a massive fuel leak and subsequent fire. Despite the crew's attempts to regain control, PSA Flight 182 entered a steep, uncontrolled descent.

The final moments of PSA Flight 182 were captured on the cockpit voice recorder (CVR). The crew's last words were a desperate attempt to communicate with air traffic control and each other as they tried to manage the rapidly deteriorating situation. At 9:02 AM, the Boeing 727 crashed into the North Park neighborhood of San Diego, approximately three miles northeast of Lindbergh Field. The impact caused a massive explosion and fireball, devastating the residential area and destroying or damaging numerous homes.

The aftermath of the collision was catastrophic. All 135 passengers and crew members on board PSA Flight 182 perished, as did the two occupants of the Cessna. On the ground, seven residents were killed, and nine others were injured. The destruction extended across a wide swath of the neighborhood, with many houses engulfed in flames and debris scattered over a large area.

The National Transportation Safety Board (NTSB) immediately launched an investigation into the crash, one of the most complex and challenging inquiries in the board's history due to the extensive damage and loss of life. The investigation team included representatives from the Federal Aviation Administration (FAA), PSA, Cessna, and other relevant parties.

The NTSB's investigation focused on several critical factors: the collision sequence, air traffic control procedures, pilot actions, and aircraft performance. The investigation revealed that the primary cause of the collision was a failure of both flight crews to maintain adequate visual separation. The PSA crew's misidentification of the Cessna as a different aircraft and the subsequent failure to visually locate and avoid the Cessna were central to the accident.

The investigation also highlighted significant shortcomings in air traffic control procedures and communications. The TRACON controller had provided traffic advisories to both aircraft but had not issued specific avoidance instructions. Furthermore, the controller's assumption that the PSA crew had correctly identified and avoided the Cessna contributed to the lack of intervention that might have prevented the collision.

The NTSB's final report, issued in April 1979, concluded that the probable cause of the accident was the failure of the flight crews of both aircraft to see and avoid each other. Contributing factors included the inherent limitations of the see-and-avoid concept, the busy airspace around San Diego, and deficiencies in air traffic control procedures. The report emphasized the need for improvements in collision avoidance technology and air traffic management.

In the wake of the PSA Flight 182 disaster, several significant changes were implemented to enhance aviation safety and prevent similar accidents. One of the most crucial developments was the accelerated deployment of the Traffic Collision Avoidance System (TCAS), a sophisticated onboard system designed to detect and alert pilots to potential mid-air collisions. TCAS provides resolution advisories that direct pilots to take specific actions to avoid collisions, significantly improving safety in busy airspace.

Additionally, the FAA revised air traffic control procedures to enhance the separation of aircraft operating in congested areas. These changes included improved training for controllers, updated communication protocols, and enhanced radar capabilities. The goal was to reduce the reliance on visual separation and provide more robust and reliable methods for ensuring aircraft remain safely apart.

The tragedy also underscored the need for better training and awareness among pilots regarding mid-air collision risks and avoidance strategies. Airlines and aviation authorities introduced more rigorous training programs focused on situational awareness, traffic management, and the effective use of collision avoidance systems.

The PSA Flight 182 disaster left a lasting impact on the San Diego community. The North Park neighborhood, which bore the brunt of the crash, underwent significant rebuilding and recovery efforts. Memorials and commemorations were established to honor the victims and provide solace to the survivors and their families. One notable memorial is located at the crash site in North Park, featuring a plaque and dedicated area for reflection and remembrance.

For the families of the victims, the aftermath of the crash was a period of profound grief and loss. Many sought answers and accountability, pushing for changes to prevent future tragedies. Their advocacy played a crucial role in driving the safety improvements that followed the disaster.

The legacy of PSA Flight 182 extends beyond the immediate changes in regulations and technology. The incident serves as a powerful reminder of the importance of vigilance, communication, and continuous improvement in aviation safety. It highlights the critical need for robust collision avoidance systems, effective air traffic management, and comprehensive pilot training.

For aviation professionals and enthusiasts, the crash of PSA Flight 182 is a sobering case study in the complexities of air traffic control and collision avoidance. It underscores the necessity of ongoing advancements in technology and procedures to ensure the safety of all who travel by air. The lessons learned from this tragedy have contributed to the development of a safer and more reliable aviation industry.

Chapter 34: Pacific Southwest Airlines Flight 1771

Pacific Southwest Airlines (PSA) Flight 1771 was a scheduled domestic passenger flight from Los Angeles International Airport (LAX) to San Francisco International Airport (SFO). On December 7, 1987, the flight ended in tragedy when it crashed near Cayucos, California, following a deliberate act of violence by a disgruntled former employee. The incident resulted in the deaths of all 43 people on board, including the perpetrator. The crash highlighted significant security vulnerabilities in the airline industry and led to important changes in aviation security protocols.

The aircraft involved in the crash was a British Aerospace BAe 146-200, a four-engine regional jet designed for short-haul flights. On the day of the incident, the flight was operated by a seasoned crew, including Captain Gregg Lindamood, First Officer James Nunn, and three flight attendants. Captain Lindamood was an experienced pilot with over 11,000 flight hours, while First Officer Nunn had accumulated over 8,000 flight hours.

The flight departed Los Angeles at approximately 3:31 PM PST, with a scheduled arrival time in San Francisco of 4:43 PM. Among the passengers was David Burke, a former employee of USAir, which had recently acquired PSA. Burke had been terminated from his job as a ticket agent for petty theft, specifically for stealing $69 from an airline fund. Despite appealing his dismissal, Burke was unsuccessful in regaining his position.

On the day of the flight, Burke purchased a ticket for Flight 1771 and used his USAir credentials to bypass the security checkpoint at LAX, which allowed him to board the aircraft with a loaded .44 Magnum revolver. This breach of security would later become a focal point in the investigation and lead to significant changes in airport security measures.

Shortly after takeoff, Burke wrote a note to his former supervisor, Raymond Thomson, who was also on board the flight. The note, written on an air sickness bag, read, "Hi Ray. I think it's sort of ironical that we ended up like this. I asked for some leniency for my family, remember? Well, I got none. And you'll get none." Burke then made his way to the cockpit area.

At approximately 4:09 PM, while the aircraft was cruising at 22,000 feet, the cockpit voice recorder (CVR) captured the sound of a gunshot in the passenger cabin. This was followed by the sound of the cockpit door opening and more gunshots, as Burke forced his way into the cockpit and shot both pilots. The CVR recorded Burke announcing, "I'm the problem," before firing more shots, presumably at the flight crew and possibly at the aircraft's control systems.

The loss of control and subsequent descent was rapid and catastrophic. The aircraft, now effectively pilotless, entered a steep dive at a speed exceeding 700 miles per hour. The G-forces from the descent caused structural failure, and the aircraft disintegrated in mid-air. Debris from the plane was scattered over a wide area near the small coastal town of Cayucos.

The crash site was located in a remote and rugged area, making recovery efforts challenging. All 43 people on board were killed instantly, and the scattered wreckage complicated the task of piecing together the events leading to the disaster. The FBI and the National Transportation Safety Board (NTSB) launched a joint investigation to determine the cause of the crash and the sequence of events.

Investigators quickly focused on the background and actions of David Burke. The discovery of the note addressed to Raymond Thomson provided a clear indication of Burke's motive. Further examination of Burke's employment history and the circumstances surrounding his termination revealed a pattern of erratic and troubling behavior. The security breach that allowed Burke to bring a loaded firearm onto the aircraft was a critical factor in the incident.

The NTSB's final report, released in September 1988, concluded that the probable cause of the crash was the intentional act of a former employee who boarded the flight with a concealed firearm and used it to fatally wound the flight crew, causing a loss of control of the aircraft. The report emphasized the need for stricter security measures to prevent similar incidents in the future.

In response to the crash of Flight 1771, significant changes were implemented in airport security protocols across the United States. One of the most immediate changes was the tightening of security screening procedures to ensure that all passengers, including airline employees, underwent thorough security checks before boarding. The use of employee credentials to bypass security checkpoints was discontinued.

Additionally, the FAA mandated the installation of fortified cockpit doors on all commercial aircraft. These reinforced doors were designed to prevent unauthorized access to the cockpit, thus enhancing the safety of the flight crew and passengers. The regulations also required that cockpit doors remain locked during flight, with access controlled solely by the flight crew.

The tragedy of Flight 1771 also led to increased scrutiny of airline personnel policies and mental health support for employees. Airlines were encouraged to implement more comprehensive background checks and to provide better support and resources for employees facing personal or professional difficulties. This included offering counseling services and establishing clear protocols for addressing behavioral concerns.

The impact of the crash extended beyond regulatory changes. It brought to light the vulnerabilities within the aviation industry and underscored the importance of maintaining robust security measures to protect passengers and crew. The incident also highlighted the devastating consequences of workplace violence and the need for effective intervention strategies.

For the families of the victims, the aftermath of the crash was a period of profound grief and loss. The sudden and violent nature of the tragedy made the grieving process particularly challenging. Memorial services and commemorations were held to honor the lives lost, and support groups were established to provide assistance to the bereaved families.

In the years following the crash, the legacy of Flight 1771 has served as a stark reminder of the need for vigilance and continuous improvement in aviation security. The changes implemented in the wake of the disaster have contributed to making air travel safer and have helped prevent similar incidents from occurring.

The crash also serves as a case study in the complexities of human behavior and the importance of addressing underlying issues that can lead to acts of violence. It underscores the need for comprehensive approaches to security that encompass not only physical measures but also psychological and social factors.

Chapter 35: Avianca Flight 52

Avianca Flight 52 was a regularly scheduled flight from Bogotá, Colombia to New York City's John F. Kennedy International Airport with a stopover in Medellín. On the evening of January 25, 1990, the Boeing 707-321B, registered as HK-2016, was operated by Avianca, the national airline of Colombia. The aircraft was carrying 158 people, including passengers and crew members. The flight, which had operated smoothly until its approach to New York, ended in tragedy when the plane crashed into the small town of Cove Neck on Long Island, New York, resulting in the deaths of 73 passengers and crew members.

The events leading up to the crash of Avianca Flight 52 began with its departure from Medellín's José María Córdova International Airport. The flight crew, consisting of Captain Laureano Caviedes, First Officer Mauricio Klotz, and Flight Engineer Dante Herrera, were experienced aviators, though the language barrier and communication issues would play a crucial role in the disaster. The flight proceeded uneventfully through Colombian airspace and into the Caribbean, where it encountered minor turbulence but nothing out of the ordinary.

As the flight neared the United States, the weather conditions began to deteriorate. The New York metropolitan area was experiencing severe winter weather, with low visibility and heavy fog. These adverse conditions caused significant delays and congestion at John F. Kennedy International Airport. Consequently, air traffic control (ATC) implemented holding patterns for incoming flights, including Avianca Flight 52. The aircraft entered its first holding pattern over Norfolk, Virginia, and subsequently held at various points as it approached New York.

During the holding patterns, the crew of Flight 52 became increasingly concerned about their fuel situation. Communication with ATC became critical as the crew sought updates and instructions. However, a series of misunderstandings and miscommunications occurred between the flight crew and air traffic controllers. The language barrier between the Spanish-speaking pilots and English-speaking controllers exacerbated these issues. The pilots repeatedly expressed their concern about fuel, but their communications did not convey the urgency of their situation effectively.

At one point, First Officer Klotz communicated with ATC, stating that they needed priority because they were "running out of fuel." However, this message did not convey the gravity of the situation, as the controllers did not interpret it as an emergency. In aviation terminology, a more urgent declaration such as "mayday" or "emergency" might have prompted a different response. The crew's failure to declare a fuel emergency in clear terms was a critical factor in the ensuing disaster.

As the aircraft continued to hold and burn fuel, the crew became increasingly desperate. The captain decided to descend and attempt a landing despite the aircraft's low fuel state. ATC vectored the flight towards JFK, but the approach was complicated by the weather conditions and the aircraft's critical fuel state. During the final approach, the aircraft experienced significant turbulence, and the crew struggled to maintain control.

In the final moments of the flight, the crew realized that they would not be able to reach the airport. The engines began to flame out due to fuel exhaustion, and the aircraft lost power. At approximately 9:34 PM, the Boeing 707 crashed into a wooded area in Cove Neck, Long Island. The impact broke the fuselage into several sections, and a post-crash fire ensued.

Rescue operations were challenging due to the crash's location and the poor weather conditions. Local residents and emergency responders rushed to the scene to assist survivors. Of the 158 people on board, 85 survived, including several who were ejected from the aircraft during the crash. The survivors were taken to nearby hospitals, and the bodies of the deceased were recovered from the wreckage.

The National Transportation Safety Board (NTSB) launched an investigation into the crash of Avianca Flight 52. The investigation revealed several key factors that contributed to the disaster. The primary cause was determined to be fuel exhaustion, which led to the engines flaming out. The NTSB's final report cited the flight crew's failure to properly communicate their fuel emergency to ATC and the controllers' failure to recognize the severity of the situation.

The investigation also highlighted issues related to cockpit resource management (CRM) and communication between the flight crew and ATC. The language barrier and the crew's failure to use standard emergency terminology were significant contributing factors. Additionally, the report noted that the holding patterns and delays imposed by ATC due to the congested airspace and weather conditions exacerbated the fuel situation.

The crash of Avianca Flight 52 led to several changes in aviation procedures and regulations. One of the most significant changes was the emphasis on improving communication between flight crews and air traffic controllers, particularly in situations involving language barriers. The importance of clear and precise communication in declaring emergencies was underscored, and training programs for pilots and controllers were updated to reflect these lessons.

Moreover, the incident highlighted the need for better fuel management practices and the importance of CRM in the cockpit. Airlines and regulatory authorities implemented measures to enhance CRM training, ensuring that flight crews could work more effectively as a team, communicate clearly, and manage in-flight emergencies more efficiently.

In the years following the crash, the aviation industry has continued to evolve, with advancements in technology, training, and communication practices. The lessons learned from the crash of Avianca Flight 52 have contributed to improving the safety and reliability of air travel, preventing similar tragedies in the future.

Despite the improvements and changes in the industry, the memories of the passengers and crew who lost their lives in the crash of Avianca Flight 52 remain poignant. Memorials and tributes have been established to honor their memory, and the event continues to serve as a reminder of the critical importance of communication, training, and vigilance in ensuring the safety of air travel.

Chapter 36: Mandala Airlines Flight 091

Mandala Airlines Flight 091 was a scheduled domestic passenger flight that crashed shortly after takeoff from Polonia International Airport in Medan, Indonesia, on September 5, 2005. The aircraft involved was a Boeing 737-230, registered PK-RIM, carrying 117 people, including passengers and crew. Tragically, 100 people on board the aircraft died, and the crash resulted in an additional 49 fatalities and numerous injuries on the ground due to the plane crashing into a densely populated residential area. The disaster is one of the deadliest aviation accidents in Indonesia's history, and it prompted significant changes in aviation safety and regulatory oversight in the country.

The flight was bound for Jakarta's Soekarno-Hatta International Airport. On the morning of the crash, the aircraft taxied out to the runway and was cleared for takeoff. Weather conditions at the time were clear, and there were no immediate indications of problems as the aircraft began its takeoff roll. However, shortly after becoming airborne, the aircraft struggled to gain altitude and began veering off course. Within moments, it struck several buildings, crashed into a busy street, and burst into flames.

Initial reports from survivors and witnesses indicated that the plane seemed to have difficulty climbing, leading investigators to consider a range of potential causes, including mechanical failure, pilot error, and weight and balance issues. The wreckage was scattered over a wide area, complicating recovery efforts and the subsequent investigation. Emergency response teams arrived quickly at the scene, but the intensity of the fire and the extent of the destruction made rescue operations challenging. Many of the victims were trapped inside the burning aircraft, and others were severely injured by debris and the post-crash fire.

The Indonesian National Transportation Safety Committee (NTSC) led the investigation, with assistance from the United States'

National Transportation Safety Board (NTSB) and Boeing. The investigation revealed several critical findings. One of the primary causes of the crash was the improper configuration of the aircraft for takeoff. Specifically, the flaps and slats, which are crucial for generating the necessary lift during takeoff, had not been extended. This oversight significantly impaired the aircraft's ability to climb.

The investigation further revealed that the takeoff warning system, designed to alert pilots if the aircraft is not properly configured for takeoff, had failed to activate. This failure was attributed to a malfunction in the system, which allowed the crew to commence the takeoff without realizing that the flaps and slats were not extended. The crew's failure to notice the improper configuration during pre-flight checks and takeoff roll was a critical error.

In addition to the configuration issues, the investigation found that the aircraft was significantly over its maximum takeoff weight. This excessive weight further compounded the difficulties in gaining altitude and controlling the aircraft. The weight and balance discrepancies were attributed to inadequate adherence to loading procedures and a lack of proper oversight by the airline.

The NTSC's final report also highlighted deficiencies in pilot training and cockpit resource management (CRM). The report noted that the pilots did not effectively communicate or cross-check critical information during the pre-flight and takeoff phases. This breakdown in communication and coordination was a significant factor in the failure to detect and correct the improper configuration and weight issues before takeoff.

In the aftermath of the crash, Mandala Airlines faced intense scrutiny and criticism. The airline was found to have systemic issues related to safety oversight, maintenance practices, and compliance with regulations. As a result, Indonesian aviation authorities implemented stricter regulations and oversight measures to address these deficiencies and prevent similar accidents in the future.

One of the immediate actions taken by Indonesian authorities was to ground Mandala Airlines' entire fleet for a comprehensive safety audit. This audit revealed numerous safety violations and deficiencies in the airline's operations, leading to significant fines and sanctions. The grounding also provided an opportunity for the airline to revamp its safety protocols, improve maintenance practices, and enhance pilot training programs.

The crash of Mandala Airlines Flight 091 also prompted broader reforms in Indonesia's aviation industry. The Indonesian Directorate General of Civil Aviation (DGCA) undertook a thorough review of its regulatory framework and oversight capabilities. The review resulted in the implementation of more stringent safety regulations, improved oversight mechanisms, and enhanced training programs for both pilots and maintenance personnel.

Furthermore, the incident underscored the importance of effective CRM and proper communication in the cockpit. Airlines across Indonesia were mandated to improve their CRM training programs to ensure that flight crews could work more cohesively and effectively manage in-flight situations. The emphasis on CRM aimed to prevent miscommunications and enhance the overall safety culture within the aviation industry.

Internationally, the crash drew attention to the importance of proper aircraft configuration and the critical role of takeoff warning systems. The aviation industry responded by re-evaluating the reliability and functionality of these systems across different aircraft types. Manufacturers and airlines collaborated to ensure that takeoff warning systems were adequately maintained and regularly tested to prevent similar failures.

In the years following the crash, Mandala Airlines made significant strides in improving its safety record and rebuilding its reputation. The airline invested heavily in new aircraft, upgraded its maintenance facilities, and implemented comprehensive training programs for its staff. These efforts were aimed at regaining the trust of passengers and regulatory authorities, and ultimately ensuring the highest standards of safety in its operations.

Despite these improvements, the memories of the victims and the impact of the crash on the Medan community remain deeply felt. Memorials and tributes have been established to honor those who lost their lives in the disaster. The crash of Mandala Airlines Flight 091 serves as a somber reminder of the critical importance of adherence to safety protocols, effective communication, and rigorous oversight in the aviation industry.

The lessons learned from the crash continue to influence aviation safety practices and regulatory frameworks worldwide. The incident has contributed to a greater understanding of the complexities of aircraft operations and the need for continuous vigilance in maintaining and enhancing safety standards. As the aviation industry evolves, the experiences and lessons from past tragedies like Mandala Airlines Flight 091 play a crucial role in shaping a safer future for air travel.

Chapter 37: Comair Flight 5191

Comair Flight 5191, also marketed as Delta Connection Flight 5191, was a scheduled domestic passenger flight from Lexington, Kentucky, to Atlanta, Georgia. On the morning of August 27, 2006, the Bombardier CRJ100ER, registered as N431CA, crashed during takeoff from Blue Grass Airport in Lexington. The aircraft, operated by Comair, was carrying 47 passengers and 3 crew members. Tragically, 49 of the 50 people on board died in the crash, with the First Officer being the sole survivor. The disaster is among the deadliest aviation accidents in U.S. history, and it led to significant changes in airport safety procedures and pilot training.

On that fateful morning, Captain Jeffrey Clay and First Officer James Polehinke were preparing for an early morning departure. The flight was scheduled to take off from Runway 22, the airport's main runway. However, due to confusion and a series of errors, the aircraft was mistakenly lined up on Runway 26, a shorter, unlit runway primarily used for general aviation. The aircraft began its takeoff roll on the incorrect runway without either pilot realizing the mistake.

Weather conditions were clear, with no significant issues that would affect visibility or operations. The aircraft taxied out to the runway and, after receiving clearance from the control tower, proceeded with the takeoff. As the CRJ100ER accelerated down Runway 26, it quickly became evident that the aircraft did not have enough runway length to achieve takeoff speed. The aircraft overran the runway, struck a perimeter fence, and crashed into a field just beyond the airport boundaries. The impact resulted in a massive fire, consuming much of the aircraft and causing catastrophic damage.

Rescue operations were initiated almost immediately by airport fire and rescue services, but the intensity of the fire and the extent of the damage made it difficult to save the passengers and crew. First Officer Polehinke, who was severely injured but survived, was rescued from the cockpit and transported to a nearby hospital for treatment. Unfortunately, all other occupants of the aircraft perished either due to the initial impact or the ensuing fire.

The National Transportation Safety Board (NTSB) launched an investigation into the crash of Comair Flight 5191, which revealed a series of critical errors and lapses in standard operating procedures. The investigation focused on several key areas, including human factors, airport layout, and procedural adherence.

One of the primary findings was the flight crew's failure to correctly identify and use the appropriate runway for takeoff. Runway 22, the designated runway for the flight, was significantly longer and equipped with the necessary lighting and markings for commercial aircraft operations. In contrast, Runway 26 was shorter and lacked proper lighting, making it unsuitable for the takeoff of a commercial jet. The investigation determined that the pilots had not adequately cross-checked their position on the airport surface against their takeoff clearance and had not confirmed their runway assignment visually.

Further compounding the error was the absence of a more robust system to prevent runway incursions and misidentifications. The Blue Grass Airport had a complex layout, with intersecting runways and taxiways that could easily lead to confusion, particularly during nighttime or low-light conditions. The lack of advanced surface movement guidance and control systems (SMGCS) contributed to the pilots' misidentification of the runway.

The investigation also highlighted deficiencies in cockpit resource management (CRM) and adherence to standard operating procedures. The flight crew failed to conduct a thorough briefing and cross-check before takeoff, which could have helped identify the error. Additionally, the pilots were found to have been engaged in non-essential conversation during taxi, which may have contributed to their loss of situational awareness.

Another significant factor identified was the role of fatigue. The flight crew had reported for duty early in the morning, following a schedule that may have contributed to cumulative fatigue. Although not definitively cited as a primary cause, fatigue was recognized as a potential contributor to the lapses in judgment and situational awareness exhibited by the pilots.

As a result of the investigation, several safety recommendations and changes were implemented to prevent similar accidents in the future. One of the most immediate actions was the installation of enhanced runway lighting and signage at Blue Grass Airport to reduce the risk of runway confusion. The airport also undertook a redesign of its taxiway and runway layout to simplify navigation and reduce the likelihood of similar errors.

On a broader scale, the Federal Aviation Administration (FAA) issued directives to improve pilot training and CRM practices. Emphasis was placed on the importance of adherence to standard operating procedures, including thorough pre-takeoff briefings and strict compliance with sterile cockpit rules, which prohibit non-essential conversation during critical phases of flight. Additionally, airlines were encouraged to adopt more rigorous fatigue management programs to ensure that flight crews are adequately rested and alert.

The FAA also mandated the implementation of advanced surface movement guidance and control systems at major airports across the United States. These systems, which include ground radar and automated alerts, help pilots and air traffic controllers monitor and manage aircraft movements on the ground, thereby reducing the risk of runway incursions and misidentifications.

In the wake of the Comair Flight 5191 disaster, the aviation industry also saw a renewed focus on human factors and the role of automation in enhancing safety. Airlines invested in advanced training programs that incorporate realistic simulations and scenario-based training to prepare pilots for a wide range of potential emergencies and operational challenges.

The legacy of Comair Flight 5191 extends beyond the immediate changes in airport infrastructure and pilot training. The tragedy underscored the critical importance of vigilance, communication, and adherence to procedures in aviation safety. It served as a stark reminder that even routine operations can quickly turn catastrophic if errors and lapses go unchecked.

For the families and loved ones of those who perished, the crash of Comair Flight 5191 remains a deeply personal and painful memory. Memorials and tributes have been established to honor the victims, and efforts continue to support the survivors and their families. The aviation community has taken these lessons to heart, striving to ensure that such a tragedy never occurs again.

Chapter 38: Air New Zealand Flight 901

Air New Zealand Flight 901, also known as TE901, was a scheduled Antarctic sightseeing flight that ended in tragedy on November 28, 1979, when it crashed into Mount Erebus on Ross Island, Antarctica. The flight was operated by a McDonnell Douglas DC-10-30 aircraft, registered as ZK-NZP, carrying 237 passengers and 20 crew members. All 257 people on board were killed in the crash, making it New Zealand's deadliest peacetime disaster. The incident led to a complex and controversial investigation, resulting in significant changes to aviation safety protocols and practices.

Flight 901 was part of a popular series of scenic flights offered by Air New Zealand, providing passengers with a unique opportunity to view the Antarctic landscape from the air. The flight departed from Auckland International Airport early in the morning, with a planned route that included several hours of flying over the Antarctic continent before returning to Christchurch. The passengers on board were mostly New Zealanders, along with some Australians and Japanese, eager to witness the breathtaking scenery of Antarctica.

The flight crew consisted of Captain Jim Collins, First Officer Greg Cassin, Flight Engineer Gordon Brooks, and two additional flight engineers. Captain Collins and First Officer Cassin were experienced pilots, but they had not previously flown the Antarctic route. To assist with navigation and provide commentary on the Antarctic landmarks, an experienced Antarctic guide, Peter Mulgrew, was also on board.

Unbeknownst to the flight crew, there had been a critical change to the flight's navigation coordinates. The flight plan originally programmed into the aircraft's navigation system had been altered the night before the flight, changing the coordinates by a small but significant margin. The original coordinates would have taken the aircraft safely over McMurdo Sound, but the new coordinates directed the aircraft toward Mount Erebus, a 3,794-meter (12,448-foot) high volcano.

As Flight 901 approached the Antarctic coast, the crew initiated a descent to provide passengers with a better view of the scenery. The weather conditions in the area were typical for Antarctica, with limited visibility due to a phenomenon known as whiteout, where the snow-covered ground blends with the overcast sky, making it difficult to discern the horizon or any obstacles. Relying on their instruments and believing they were on a safe course over McMurdo Sound, the crew continued their descent.

In reality, the aircraft was on a collision course with Mount Erebus. The flight crew, unaware of the incorrect coordinates, did not recognize the danger. As the DC-10 descended to an altitude of approximately 1,500 feet (460 meters), it entered a layer of cloud, further reducing visibility. At 12:49 PM, the aircraft struck the lower slopes of Mount Erebus, traveling at a speed of 260 knots (480 km/h; 300 mph). The impact and subsequent fire instantly killed all 257 people on board.

The wreckage of Flight 901 was discovered the following day by search and rescue teams. The harsh Antarctic environment and the remote location of the crash site made recovery operations extremely challenging. The wreckage was scattered across the slopes of Mount Erebus, and many bodies were buried under snow and ice. Despite these difficulties, recovery teams worked tirelessly to retrieve the remains of the victims and investigate the cause of the crash.

The initial investigation into the disaster was conducted by the New Zealand Ministry of Transport's Chief Inspector of Air Accidents, Ron Chippindale. His report, released in 1980, concluded that the probable cause of the accident was pilot error, specifically the decision to descend below the minimum safe altitude in poor visibility. The report also cited the crew's failure to recognize the navigational error and their reliance on visual flight rules (VFR) in conditions that required instrument flight rules (IFR).

Chippindale's findings were met with significant controversy and public outcry, particularly from the families of the victims and the New Zealand pilots' association. They argued that the report unfairly blamed the flight crew and did not adequately address systemic issues within Air New Zealand and the role of the navigational error.

In response to the public outcry, the New Zealand government appointed a Royal Commission of Inquiry, headed by Justice Peter Mahon, to conduct an independent investigation into the crash. Justice Mahon's inquiry delved deeper into the circumstances surrounding the flight and the events leading up to the disaster. His findings, released in 1981, dramatically contradicted the initial investigation's conclusions.

Justice Mahon's report identified the primary cause of the crash as the incorrect coordinates in the flight plan, which had been changed without the knowledge of the flight crew. He argued that the crew had been misled by the erroneous navigation data and that their descent was consistent with the belief that they were flying over safe terrain. Justice Mahon also criticized Air New Zealand for its inadequate training and briefing procedures for the Antarctic flights, as well as its failure to inform the crew of the coordinate change.

One of the most controversial aspects of Justice Mahon's report was his accusation of a cover-up by Air New Zealand and certain officials involved in the initial investigation. He famously described the conduct of these officials as an "orchestrated litany of lies." This phrase became synonymous with the Erebus disaster and highlighted the perceived attempts to shift blame onto the flight crew while concealing systemic failings within the airline and the aviation authorities.

The findings of the Royal Commission of Inquiry had profound implications for aviation safety and regulatory practices in New Zealand and internationally. Air New Zealand implemented significant changes to its procedures, including improved training for Antarctic operations, more rigorous pre-flight briefings, and enhanced oversight of flight planning and navigation data. The airline also introduced measures to ensure better communication and coordination between flight crews and ground support personnel.

The Erebus disaster also led to changes in the broader aviation industry, particularly regarding the importance of accurate navigation data and the need for robust systems to prevent similar errors. The incident underscored the critical role of human factors in aviation safety and the necessity of addressing systemic issues rather than solely attributing accidents to pilot error.

In the years following the Erebus disaster, the memory of those who perished has been honored through various memorials and commemorations. A memorial cross was erected on the slopes of Mount Erebus, and a memorial garden was established in Auckland, providing a place for families and loved ones to remember the victims. Annual commemorative events are held to mark the anniversary of the crash, reflecting the lasting impact of the tragedy on New Zealand society.

The legacy of Air New Zealand Flight 901 extends beyond the immediate changes to aviation safety practices. The disaster and the subsequent investigations highlighted the importance of transparency, accountability, and a commitment to continuous improvement in the aviation industry. The lessons learned from the Erebus disaster continue to influence safety protocols and regulatory frameworks, contributing to the ongoing efforts to enhance the safety and reliability of air travel.

Chapter 39: Qantas Flight 32

Qantas Flight 32, an international passenger flight from London Heathrow to Sydney, experienced a catastrophic engine failure shortly after taking off from Singapore's Changi Airport on November 4, 2010. The aircraft involved was an Airbus A380-842, the world's largest passenger airliner, registered as VH-OQA and named Nancy-Bird Walton after the pioneering Australian aviator. The flight was operated by Qantas, Australia's flag carrier, and carried 440 passengers and 29 crew members. The incident was unprecedented in its complexity and severity, yet it resulted in no fatalities, showcasing the extraordinary skills of the flight crew and the robust safety design of the aircraft.

On the day of the incident, Qantas Flight 32 departed from London and landed in Singapore for a scheduled stopover. The crew consisted of Captain Richard de Crespigny, First Officer Matt Hicks, Second Officer Mark Johnson, and two additional relief pilots, David Evans and Harry Wubben. The A380 took off from Singapore at approximately 9:56 AM local time, heading towards Sydney. About four minutes after takeoff, as the aircraft was climbing through 7,000 feet, the number two engine, one of four Rolls-Royce Trent 900 engines, suffered an uncontained failure.

The failure occurred when a turbine disc in the engine disintegrated, sending shrapnel through the wing and fuselage. This caused significant damage to the aircraft, including the rupture of fuel lines, the severing of hydraulic and electrical systems, and the loss of multiple flight control systems. The explosion also caused a fire in the wing, which was quickly extinguished by the aircraft's automated fire suppression systems. The passengers and crew heard a loud bang and felt a noticeable jolt, followed by a series of system warnings and alarms in the cockpit.

Captain de Crespigny and his team were immediately faced with a barrage of error messages, as the aircraft's systems tried to cope with the extensive damage. The Electronic Centralized Aircraft Monitor (ECAM) displayed over 50 warnings and advisories, indicating failures in the fuel, hydraulic, and electrical systems, as well as issues with flight controls and engine thrust. The sheer number of alerts and the complexity of the situation were unprecedented, requiring the flight crew to prioritize and manage multiple failures simultaneously.

The pilots declared an emergency and requested to return to Singapore. Despite the overwhelming number of failures, the crew remained calm and methodical. They worked through the ECAM procedures to assess and manage the damage, while also communicating with Qantas operations and air traffic control. One of the critical challenges was managing the aircraft's weight and balance, as the damage had caused fuel to leak from the damaged wing, altering the aircraft's center of gravity.

The flight crew decided to dump fuel to reduce the aircraft's weight for landing, a standard procedure in emergencies. However, the damage to the fuel systems made this process difficult and time-consuming. The crew had to manually manage the fuel transfer and dumping, a task that required precise coordination and monitoring. Meanwhile, they continued to troubleshoot the multiple systems failures and prepare for a potential emergency landing.

As the situation unfolded, the cabin crew, led by Customer Service Manager Michael von Reth, played a crucial role in managing the passengers. They reassured the passengers, provided regular updates, and ensured that everyone was prepared for an emergency landing. The professionalism and calm demeanor of the cabin crew helped to maintain order and prevent panic among the passengers.

After nearly two hours of managing the emergency in the air, the flight crew was finally ready to attempt a landing. They aligned the aircraft for an approach to Runway 20C at Changi Airport. Given the extensive damage to the aircraft, including the loss of several braking and flight control systems, the landing was expected to be challenging.

The pilots performed a flawless approach and landing, bringing the heavily damaged A380 to a stop on the runway.

Upon landing, the aircraft's brakes were found to be inoperative due to the severed hydraulic lines, and the pilots had to rely on reverse thrust and the remaining functioning systems to bring the aircraft to a stop. Emergency services at Changi Airport were on high alert and quickly surrounded the aircraft, ready to respond to any further incidents. Fortunately, there were no fires or additional damage upon landing, and all passengers and crew were safely evacuated.

The aftermath of the incident involved a detailed investigation by the Australian Transport Safety Bureau (ATSB), with assistance from Airbus, Rolls-Royce, and other aviation authorities. The investigation revealed that the engine failure was caused by a manufacturing defect in an oil feed pipe, which led to a crack and subsequent oil leak. The leaking oil ignited and caused the turbine disc to disintegrate, resulting in the uncontained engine failure.

The ATSB's final report, released in 2013, made several key findings and recommendations. The report highlighted the need for improved manufacturing processes and quality control measures at Rolls-Royce to prevent similar defects in the future. It also recommended enhancements to the A380's design and maintenance procedures to improve its resilience to uncontained engine failures.

In response to the incident, Rolls-Royce undertook a comprehensive review of its Trent 900 engine manufacturing and inspection processes. The company implemented several changes to address the issues identified in the investigation, including more rigorous quality control measures and improved materials testing procedures. Airbus also made modifications to the A380's design and maintenance protocols to enhance its safety and reliability.

Qantas, for its part, conducted an extensive review of its safety and emergency procedures. The airline reinforced its training programs for pilots and cabin crew, focusing on managing complex emergencies and improving coordination and communication during crises. The successful handling of the Flight 32 incident was widely praised, and Captain de Crespigny and his crew received numerous awards and accolades for their professionalism and skill.

The incident also had a broader impact on the aviation industry, prompting regulatory authorities to review and update safety standards for large commercial aircraft. The lessons learned from Qantas Flight 32 contributed to ongoing efforts to enhance the safety and resilience of the global aviation system.

In the years since the incident, Qantas Flight 32 has been studied extensively as a case study in aviation safety and crisis management. The event underscored the importance of thorough training, effective communication, and the ability to remain calm and focused under pressure. It also highlighted the resilience of modern aircraft design and the critical role of robust safety systems in preventing disasters.

For the passengers and crew of Qantas Flight 32, the incident was a harrowing experience that left a lasting impression. Many passengers later recounted their gratitude for the professionalism and care shown by the flight and cabin crew, who managed to avert a potential catastrophe. The successful outcome of the incident stands as a testament to the skill and dedication of aviation professionals and the importance of continuous improvement in safety practices.

Chapter 40: Pan Am Flight 6

Pan American World Airways Flight 6, also known as Pan Am Flight 6, was a scheduled round-the-world flight that encountered a critical emergency on the night of October 16, 1956. The flight, operating from Philadelphia to Honolulu via several stops, was serviced by a Boeing 377 Stratocruiser, registered as N90943 and named "Clipper Sovereign of the Skies." On this particular leg of its journey, from Honolulu to San Francisco, the aircraft experienced a severe mechanical failure that resulted in one of the most dramatic and well-documented ocean ditchings in aviation history. The successful ditching and subsequent rescue of all on board highlighted the skill and bravery of the flight crew and rescuers.

The Boeing 377 Stratocruiser was a large, propeller-driven aircraft developed by Boeing in the late 1940s, known for its distinctive double-deck design and luxurious accommodations. It was a workhorse for long-haul international flights in the early years of commercial aviation, prized for its range and passenger comfort.

Pan Am Flight 6 was under the command of Captain Olof E. "Ole" Jorgensen, an experienced pilot with numerous hours of flying experience, and First Officer George L. Haaker. The flight engineer, Frank Garcia, and navigator, Dick Brown, made up the rest of the cockpit crew. The aircraft departed from Honolulu at 8:25 PM HST with 31 passengers and 8 crew members on board. The flight was expected to reach San Francisco after a journey of approximately nine hours.

Approximately halfway into the flight, over the vast expanse of the Pacific Ocean, the aircraft encountered significant mechanical problems. At around 11:30 PM HST, while cruising at 21,000 feet, the number one engine (the outer engine on the left wing) began to fail. The propeller of the malfunctioning engine could not be feathered, which means it could not be adjusted to reduce drag by aligning the blades with the airflow. Instead, the windmilling propeller created significant drag, causing the aircraft to lose altitude and increasing the strain on the remaining three engines.

Despite the crew's best efforts to manage the situation, the Stratocruiser continued to lose altitude. To make matters worse, the number four engine (the outer engine on the right wing) also began to exhibit problems, severely compromising the aircraft's performance. With two engines out and the aircraft steadily losing altitude, Captain Jorgensen realized that they could not reach their intended destination or any landmass and prepared for an emergency ocean ditching.

Jorgensen radioed a distress call to the Coast Guard, which was received by the United States Coast Guard cutter Pontchartrain, stationed as an ocean weather ship approximately 563 miles northeast of Honolulu. The Pontchartrain was equipped with radar and radio equipment, and its crew quickly began to assist with navigation and prepare for a potential rescue operation. The coordination between the aircraft and the cutter was critical in ensuring the ditching occurred as safely as possible.

As the aircraft descended towards the ocean, Captain Jorgensen briefed the passengers and crew on the emergency procedures for ditching. The flight attendants helped secure the passengers and ensured that everyone donned life vests. Jorgensen also jettisoned fuel to reduce the risk of fire upon impact and lighten the aircraft.

At approximately 8:15 AM HST on October 17, with daylight providing better visibility, Captain Jorgensen prepared for the ditching. The Pontchartrain had established visual and radio contact with the aircraft, guiding it towards a suitable ditching location near the ship. The Stratocruiser made a controlled descent, and at around 8:23 AM HST, it touched down on the ocean surface in a textbook ditching maneuver.

The impact with the water was relatively smooth, and the aircraft remained intact. The well-executed ditching was a testament to

Jorgensen's skill and experience, and the preparedness of the entire crew. The passengers and crew evacuated the aircraft in an orderly manner, using the life rafts that had been deployed. The entire ditching and evacuation process was completed without panic, greatly aided by the clear instructions and leadership of the flight crew.

Within minutes of the ditching, the rescue operation commenced. The Pontchartrain had deployed boats to assist the survivors, and the calm sea conditions facilitated the rescue efforts. All 39 occupants of the aircraft were safely transferred to the Pontchartrain, where they received medical attention and support. Remarkably, there were no fatalities or serious injuries among the passengers and crew, a rare and fortunate outcome in such a situation.

The successful ditching and rescue were widely covered by the media and praised by aviation experts. The incident highlighted several key factors that contributed to the positive outcome: the professionalism and calm demeanor of the flight crew, the effective coordination with the Coast Guard, and the preparedness and discipline of the passengers.

The subsequent investigation into the incident by the Civil Aeronautics Board (CAB) revealed that the primary cause of the engine failure was a mechanical defect in the number one engine. The inability to feather the propeller exacerbated the situation, leading to the eventual failure of the number four engine due to the increased strain. The investigation also praised Captain Jorgensen and his crew for their exceptional handling of the emergency and their successful execution of the ditching procedure.

The Pan Am Flight 6 incident had a lasting impact on aviation safety and emergency procedures. It underscored the importance of thorough training for pilots and flight crews in handling in-flight emergencies and ditching scenarios. The successful outcome demonstrated that with proper preparation, training, and coordination, even the most challenging situations could be managed effectively.

In the aftermath of the incident, Pan American World Airways reviewed and updated its emergency procedures and training programs to incorporate the lessons learned from Flight 6. The airline emphasized the importance of communication, coordination, and preparedness in dealing with in-flight emergencies. The successful ditching of Flight 6 became a case study in aviation safety, used in training programs to illustrate best practices in emergency management.

The crew members, particularly Captain Jorgensen, were commended for their exceptional performance. Jorgensen received numerous accolades and awards for his heroism and skill, and he became a celebrated figure in the aviation community. The passengers also expressed their gratitude for the professionalism and care shown by the crew during the harrowing experience.

The incident also highlighted the critical role of search and rescue operations and the importance of having well-equipped and strategically positioned assets like the Coast Guard cutter Pontchartrain. The successful coordination between the aircraft and the cutter was a key factor in the safe rescue of all on board.

The story of Pan Am Flight 6 remains a remarkable example of crisis management and a testament to the resilience and professionalism of those involved. It serves as a reminder of the inherent risks of aviation and the importance of continuous improvement in safety practices and training. The legacy of Flight 6 lives on in the ongoing efforts to enhance the safety and reliability of air travel, ensuring that the lessons learned continue to benefit future generations of aviators and passengers.

Chapter 41: Air Canada Flight 797

Air Canada Flight 797, a McDonnell Douglas DC-9-32, was on a routine international journey from Dallas/Fort Worth International Airport to Montréal–Dorval International Airport, with an intermediate stop at Toronto Pearson International Airport, on June 2, 1983. The flight took an unexpected and tragic turn when an in-flight fire broke out, leading to one of the most harrowing and significant incidents in aviation history. The catastrophe claimed the lives of 23 of the 46 people on board and led to substantial changes in aviation safety regulations, particularly concerning fire detection, suppression, and evacuation procedures.

The aircraft, registered as C-FTLU, was under the command of Captain Donald Cameron and First Officer Claude Ouimet, both experienced pilots with thousands of flight hours between them. Flight 797 departed Dallas/Fort Worth on schedule at 4:25 PM Central Daylight Time (CDT), carrying 41 passengers and 5 crew members, including three flight attendants: Laura Kay Davis, Judi Davidson, and Sergio Benetti.

Approximately 60 minutes into the flight, at an altitude of 33,000 feet, passengers seated near the rear of the aircraft began to notice an unusual odor resembling an electrical fire. Around the same time, smoke started to seep into the cabin, particularly noticeable in the aft lavatory. The source of the fire, as later investigations would reveal, was behind the wall of the rear lavatory, where a malfunction in the aircraft's electrical system ignited the fire.

As the smoke intensified, flight attendants attempted to locate and extinguish the fire using onboard extinguishers. However, the fire was hidden behind panels, making it difficult to access. Meanwhile, the smoke detectors, which were not required in the lavatories of aircraft at that time, failed to provide an early warning. As the situation deteriorated, the cabin began to fill with dense, toxic smoke, causing panic among the passengers.

Captain Cameron and First Officer Ouimet, upon being informed of the smoke in the cabin, initiated emergency procedures. At approximately 6:33 PM CDT, they declared an emergency and requested an immediate descent and diversion to the nearest suitable airport. The Louisville Standiford Field in Kentucky was quickly identified as the closest viable option for an emergency landing.

During the rapid descent, the situation in the cabin worsened dramatically. The thick smoke reduced visibility to nearly zero and made breathing increasingly difficult. Flight attendants distributed wet towels to passengers to help them breathe and instructed them to keep their heads low to avoid the densest smoke. The passengers' fear and anxiety grew as the fire, fueled by the aircraft's materials, continued to spread.

Despite the chaotic and terrifying conditions, Captain Cameron and First Officer Ouimet managed to maintain control of the aircraft and prepared for an emergency landing. The pilots faced a critical challenge: balancing the need for a rapid descent to the safety of the ground against the structural integrity and safety of the aircraft. The toxic smoke and potential fire damage posed a significant risk of structural failure.

At 6:56 PM CDT, approximately 25 minutes after the fire was first detected, Flight 797 landed at Louisville Standiford Field. The pilots executed a successful emergency landing and brought the aircraft to a stop on the runway. However, the situation remained dire. The intense heat and smoke severely compromised the structural integrity of the aircraft, making an immediate evacuation imperative.

As soon as the aircraft came to a halt, the flight attendants began the evacuation process. They opened the emergency exits and deployed the slides. However, the dense smoke and disorientation caused by the dark, toxic environment in the cabin made it challenging for passengers to locate and use the exits efficiently. Despite the flight attendants' efforts to guide and assist the passengers, the chaotic and panicked environment slowed the evacuation.

Just 90 seconds after the aircraft came to a stop, the interior was engulfed in flames. The fire had rapidly intensified, fueled by the aircraft's materials, including seat cushions and interior paneling, which released deadly gases when burned. Although many passengers managed to escape, 23 people were unable to evacuate in time and perished in the fire. The intensity of the fire was such that it consumed much of the fuselage, leaving a charred skeleton of the once intact DC-9.

In the immediate aftermath, the survivors, many suffering from smoke inhalation and burns, were treated by emergency responders. The tragic loss of life and the dramatic images of the burnt aircraft drew significant media attention and prompted a thorough investigation by aviation authorities.

The National Transportation Safety Board (NTSB) launched an extensive investigation into the causes and circumstances of the accident. The NTSB's final report, released in 1984, identified several critical factors that contributed to the severity of the incident. The primary cause of the fire was traced to a faulty electrical component in the lavatory, which ignited materials behind the lavatory wall. The fire spread undetected due to the lack of smoke detectors in the lavatory and the inability of the crew to access and extinguish the hidden fire.

The NTSB report also highlighted the significant delay in detecting the fire and the rapid spread of toxic smoke, which overwhelmed the cabin and hampered the evacuation. The materials used in the aircraft's interior, including seat cushions and wall panels, were found to release highly toxic fumes when burned, contributing to the high number of fatalities.

Based on the findings, the NTSB made several critical recommendations to improve aviation safety. These included the mandatory installation of smoke detectors in aircraft lavatories, the use of more fire-resistant materials in aircraft interiors, and the improvement of fire suppression systems. The NTSB also recommended enhanced training for flight crews on emergency procedures for in-flight fires and evacuations.

The Federal Aviation Administration (FAA) and other regulatory bodies around the world took swift action in response to the NTSB's recommendations. New regulations were implemented, mandating the installation of smoke detectors in lavatories and requiring aircraft manufacturers to use fire-resistant materials in cabin interiors. Additionally, airlines were required to improve crew training for handling in-flight fires and emergency evacuations.

One of the most significant changes resulting from the Air Canada Flight 797 tragedy was the development and implementation of improved emergency lighting and signage systems. These systems were designed to enhance passengers' ability to locate exits in low-visibility conditions, such as those caused by smoke. The improved lighting and signage have since become standard safety features in commercial aircraft.

The legacy of Air Canada Flight 797 extends beyond regulatory changes and safety improvements. The incident served as a stark reminder of the potential dangers of in-flight fires and the importance of preparedness and rapid response. The lessons learned from Flight 797 have been integrated into the training programs for pilots, flight attendants, and emergency responders, ensuring that the aviation industry is better equipped to handle similar emergencies in the future.

In addition to the technical and regulatory changes, the Air Canada Flight 797 disaster had a profound impact on the families of the victims and the survivors. The tragedy brought attention to the emotional and psychological toll of aviation accidents, leading to increased support services for those affected by such incidents. Counseling and support programs for survivors and victims' families became more common, recognizing the need for comprehensive care in the aftermath of aviation disasters.

The flight crew, particularly Captain Cameron and First Officer Ouimet, were recognized for their efforts to manage the emergency and ensure the safety of as many passengers as possible. Their actions, despite the overwhelming challenges, demonstrated the critical importance of training, experience, and composure in crisis situations. The flight attendants' bravery and dedication in assisting passengers under dire conditions were also widely acknowledged.

Chapter 42: Trans World Airlines Flight 2

Trans World Airlines (TWA) Flight 2, operating as part of the airline's regular coast-to-coast service from Los Angeles, California to New York City, experienced one of the most infamous mid-air collisions in aviation history on June 30, 1956. This tragic incident, which involved a United Airlines Douglas DC-7, took place over the Grand Canyon and resulted in the deaths of all 128 passengers and crew on both aircraft. The disaster led to significant changes in air traffic control (ATC) procedures and the modernization of airspace regulations, laying the groundwork for the advanced systems in place today.

TWA Flight 2, a Lockheed L-1049 Super Constellation, was captained by Jack Gandy, an experienced pilot with extensive flight hours. On the day of the accident, the flight departed Los Angeles International Airport (LAX) at 9:01 AM Pacific Time, bound for Kansas City and then onward to New York. The aircraft carried 64 passengers and six crew members, a typical load for this transcontinental route.

Meanwhile, United Airlines Flight 718, a Douglas DC-7, was also en route from Los Angeles to Chicago, departing LAX at 9:04 AM. This flight, commanded by Captain Robert Shirley, had 53 passengers and five crew members on board. Both flights were operating under Visual Flight Rules (VFR), a common practice at the time for transcontinental flights, which allowed pilots to navigate based on visual landmarks rather than solely relying on instruments and air traffic control guidance.

The weather on that fateful day was generally clear with scattered clouds, providing good visibility for VFR operations. However, both flights were scheduled to pass through an area with intermittent cloud cover over the Grand Canyon, a location known for its challenging airspace due to the popular tourist overflights and its varying terrain.

As both aircraft approached the Grand Canyon area, they were following their respective planned routes. TWA Flight 2 had requested a deviation from its initial flight path to avoid the clouds and turbulence, a routine request granted by ATC. United Flight 718 also made a similar request to deviate for better flying conditions. These requests set the stage for the tragedy that would unfold.

At approximately 10:30 AM, the two aircraft collided at an altitude of about 21,000 feet, directly over the Grand Canyon. The impact was catastrophic, resulting in the immediate disintegration of both aircraft. The TWA Super Constellation's left wing was sheared off, causing it to spiral uncontrollably before crashing into the canyon below. The United DC-7 suffered severe damage to its front fuselage and right wing, also leading to an uncontrollable descent and subsequent crash.

The collision site, deep within the rugged terrain of the Grand Canyon, made the recovery operations extremely challenging. Initial efforts were focused on locating the wreckage and recovering any possible survivors, but it quickly became evident that there were no survivors. The National Park Service, along with military and civilian volunteers, undertook the grim task of recovering the bodies and identifying the remains of the victims, which took several weeks due to the inaccessible crash sites and the condition of the wreckage.

The Civil Aeronautics Board (CAB), the predecessor to the National Transportation Safety Board (NTSB), launched an extensive investigation to determine the cause of the collision. The CAB's inquiry focused on several critical aspects, including the flight paths, ATC communications, and the regulations governing VFR operations. Investigators pieced together the events leading up to the collision by analyzing radar data, flight plans, and the recovered wreckage.

The CAB's final report, released in 1957, concluded that the primary cause of the collision was the limitations of the see-and-avoid concept under VFR conditions. The report highlighted that both aircraft were flying in unrestricted airspace, relying on visual separation without the benefit of radar coverage or direct ATC intervention. The deviation requests, although routine, placed the aircraft on converging flight paths at the same altitude, increasing the likelihood of a mid-air collision.

One of the key findings of the investigation was the need for improved air traffic control systems and procedures to manage the growing volume of commercial air traffic. The CAB recommended several measures to enhance aviation safety, including the expansion of radar coverage, mandatory use of Instrument Flight Rules (IFR) for certain airspace, and improved communication and coordination between ATC centers. These recommendations were aimed at reducing the reliance on visual separation and increasing the ability of controllers to monitor and manage aircraft movements more effectively.

The TWA Flight 2 and United Flight 718 collision had a profound impact on the aviation industry, prompting a comprehensive overhaul of the United States air traffic control system. The Federal Aviation Administration (FAA), established in 1958 partly in response to the Grand Canyon disaster, took immediate steps to implement the CAB's recommendations. The FAA expanded the use of radar in en route and terminal airspace, enhancing the ability of controllers to track and manage aircraft.

The incident also led to the introduction of more stringent requirements for pilots to operate under IFR in certain airspace and conditions. This shift from VFR to IFR operations significantly reduced the risk of mid-air collisions by ensuring that aircraft were separated by controllers based on precise radar data rather than relying solely on visual cues.

Another significant outcome of the collision was the development and implementation of the Air Traffic Control Radar Beacon System

(ATCRBS), also known as secondary radar. This technology allowed for more accurate tracking of aircraft equipped with transponders, providing controllers with vital information about an aircraft's position, altitude, and identification. The ATCRBS became a cornerstone of modern air traffic management, enhancing situational awareness and safety.

The Grand Canyon collision also underscored the need for improved pilot training and standard operating procedures. Airlines and regulatory bodies introduced comprehensive training programs focused on IFR operations, collision avoidance techniques, and the use of onboard navigation and communication equipment. These training initiatives were designed to equip pilots with the skills and knowledge needed to operate safely in increasingly complex and congested airspace.

In addition to technical and procedural changes, the TWA Flight 2 and United Flight 718 disaster had a lasting impact on aviation safety culture. The incident highlighted the importance of proactive risk management and the need for continuous improvement in safety practices. Airlines, regulatory authorities, and aviation organizations adopted a more collaborative approach to safety, emphasizing the sharing of information, best practices, and lessons learned from accidents and incidents.

The legacy of the Grand Canyon collision extends to the present day, influencing ongoing efforts to enhance aviation safety. The principles and practices established in the aftermath of the disaster continue to shape the policies and procedures that govern modern air travel. The emphasis on technology, training, and regulation has created a safer and more reliable aviation system, reducing the likelihood of similar tragedies in the future.

The victims of TWA Flight 2 and United Flight 718 are commemorated in various memorials, including a plaque at the Grand Canyon National Park. These memorials serve as a poignant reminder of the lives lost and the enduring impact of the disaster on the aviation industry. The memory of the collision and its aftermath underscores the importance of vigilance, innovation, and collaboration in the ongoing pursuit of aviation safety.

Chapter 43: LAPA Flight 3142

LAPA Flight 3142, a domestic flight operated by Líneas Aéreas Privadas Argentinas (LAPA), met with a catastrophic accident on August 31, 1999. The Boeing 737-204C aircraft, registration LV-WRZ, was scheduled to fly from Jorge Newbery Airport in Buenos Aires to Ingeniero Aeronáutico Ambrosio L.V. Taravella International Airport in Córdoba, Argentina. The crash resulted in the deaths of 65 of the 100 people on board, including passengers and crew, as well as two people on the ground. The subsequent investigation uncovered serious deficiencies in LAPA's operational practices and regulatory oversight, leading to substantial reforms in Argentine aviation safety regulations.

On the evening of August 31, 1999, LAPA Flight 3142 was under the command of Captain Gustavo Weigel and First Officer Luis Etcheverry, with 93 passengers and 5 crew members on board. The aircraft, a Boeing 737-200, was one of the many workhorses of the LAPA fleet, having been in service since its manufacture in 1970. The weather conditions were clear, with good visibility, typical of a late winter evening in Buenos Aires.

The pre-flight preparations appeared routine, and the aircraft was cleared for takeoff from Runway 13 at Jorge Newbery Airport. However, as the aircraft accelerated down the runway, it became evident that something was seriously wrong. The aircraft failed to achieve the necessary lift to become airborne and overshot the runway. The Boeing 737 careened off the runway, crashing through the airport perimeter fence, crossing a busy road, and finally colliding with construction equipment and a gas station, which resulted in a massive explosion and fire.

The immediate aftermath was chaotic. The aircraft broke apart, and the fire engulfed the wreckage, making rescue operations extremely difficult. Emergency response teams arrived swiftly, but the intense heat and flames hampered their efforts to reach survivors. Despite these challenges, many passengers managed to escape through emergency exits, some with the help of heroic actions from fellow passengers and crew. Tragically, 65 lives were lost, including Captain Weigel and First Officer Etcheverry, who perished in the fire. The survivors suffered various degrees of injury, from minor burns and smoke inhalation to severe trauma.

The Argentine aviation authorities, along with the National Transportation Safety Board (NTSB) of the United States and Boeing representatives, launched an extensive investigation to determine the causes of the accident. The investigation focused on several critical areas: pilot actions, aircraft systems, maintenance records, and the operational practices of LAPA.

One of the key findings of the investigation was that the aircraft had taken off with its flaps and slats retracted. These components are essential for generating additional lift during takeoff, particularly for an aircraft of the 737's size. The lack of extended flaps and slats meant that the aircraft could not achieve the necessary aerodynamic lift to become airborne, resulting in the overrun.

The investigation revealed that the takeoff warning system, which should have alerted the pilots to the incorrect configuration, had not activated. This system is designed to provide an audible alert if the aircraft is not correctly configured for takeoff. The absence of this critical warning was a significant factor in the accident.

Further scrutiny of the cockpit voice recorder (CVR) and flight data recorder (FDR) indicated that there was a breakdown in standard operating procedures and crew coordination. The CVR transcript showed that the pilots had been engaged in non-operational conversation during critical phases of the pre-flight checks and takeoff roll. This distraction likely contributed to the failure to notice the incorrect flap setting and the absence of the takeoff warning horn.

Additionally, the investigation uncovered systemic issues within LAPA's operational practices and regulatory oversight. There was evidence of inadequate training and a lack of adherence to established safety protocols. The airline had a history of non-compliance with safety regulations, and the oversight by Argentine aviation authorities was found to be insufficient.

The accident report, released by the Junta de Investigaciones de Accidentes de Aviación Civil (JIAAC), highlighted several key deficiencies:

1. **Pilot Error**: The pilots failed to properly configure the aircraft for takeoff, and their non-adherence to standard operating procedures and distraction from non-essential conversation contributed to the accident.
2. **Failure of the Takeoff Warning System**: The takeoff warning system did not activate as it should have, failing to alert the crew to the improper configuration.
3. **Inadequate Training and Oversight**: LAPA's training programs were found to be inadequate, and there was insufficient regulatory oversight to ensure compliance with safety standards.
4. **Organizational Culture**: The investigation revealed a poor safety culture within LAPA, characterized by a lack of discipline and adherence to safety protocols.

The fallout from the LAPA Flight 3142 disaster was significant. The findings led to a thorough review and overhaul of aviation safety regulations and oversight in Argentina. The Argentine government took several steps to address the identified deficiencies:

1. **Improved Regulatory Oversight**: The Argentine aviation authorities enhanced their oversight capabilities, including more rigorous inspections and enforcement of safety regulations.
2. **Enhanced Pilot Training**: New training programs were

developed to emphasize the importance of adherence to standard operating procedures and the critical role of crew resource management (CRM) in ensuring flight safety.

3. **Takeoff Warning Systems**: The incident highlighted the importance of reliable takeoff warning systems. Airlines were required to ensure these systems were fully functional and maintained to the highest standards.

4. **Safety Culture**: Efforts were made to improve the overall safety culture within airlines operating in Argentina. This included promoting a culture of safety and accountability, where adherence to safety protocols was prioritized.

The families of the victims and the survivors of LAPA Flight 3142 also sought justice and accountability. Legal actions were taken against LAPA and Argentine aviation authorities, leading to several court cases and settlements. The tragedy brought to light the need for better support systems for victims' families and more transparent processes for addressing aviation accidents.

In the years following the accident, LAPA faced significant challenges, including financial difficulties and reputational damage. The airline struggled to recover from the incident and the subsequent regulatory scrutiny. Eventually, LAPA ceased operations in 2003, a casualty of both the direct impact of the Flight 3142 disaster and broader economic difficulties in Argentina.

The legacy of LAPA Flight 3142 extends beyond the immediate regulatory changes and the closure of the airline. The incident serves as a somber reminder of the critical importance of safety in aviation. The lessons learned from the accident have been integrated into global aviation safety practices, contributing to the continuous improvement of safety standards and protocols.

Chapter 44: TAM Airlines Flight 3054

TAM Airlines Flight 3054 was a scheduled domestic passenger flight from Porto Alegre to São Paulo, Brazil. On July 17, 2007, the Airbus A320 operating the flight crashed while attempting to land at São Paulo's Congonhas Airport, resulting in the deadliest aviation accident in Brazil's history.

On that fateful day, the flight took off from Salgado Filho International Airport in Porto Alegre at 17:19 local time. The aircraft, an Airbus A320-233 registered as PR-MBK, was relatively new, having been delivered to TAM Airlines in 1998. The flight was routine until its approach to Congonhas Airport, one of São Paulo's busiest airports and known for its short runways and challenging landing conditions, especially in wet weather.

As Flight 3054 approached Congonhas Airport, the weather was poor, with rain making the runway slick. This would play a critical role in the events that followed. The airport's runway 35L had been resurfaced recently, but the new surface did not yet have grooves to help drain water and improve aircraft braking performance in wet conditions. This lack of grooving meant that the runway was particularly slippery, creating a hazardous environment for landing aircraft.

During the approach, the crew of Flight 3054 was cleared to land on runway 35L. As the aircraft touched down, it became evident that something was wrong. The plane failed to decelerate as expected and instead continued at high speed along the runway. The Airbus A320 veered to the left, crossing a busy road, and collided with a TAM Express building and a gas station just beyond the airport perimeter. The resulting explosion and fire were catastrophic.

All 187 passengers and crew members on board were killed, along with 12 people on the ground. The crash site was engulfed in flames, making rescue operations extremely difficult. The severity of the impact and the subsequent fire obliterated the aircraft, leaving only charred remains and a smoldering wreckage.

The investigation into the crash, led by the Brazilian Air Force's Aeronautical Accidents Investigation and Prevention Center (CENIPA), revealed several contributing factors. One of the primary causes identified was the improper configuration of the aircraft's thrust levers during landing. The Airbus A320 is equipped with a unique system called the "FADEC" (Full Authority Digital Engine Control), which manages the engines' performance. It was found that one of the thrust levers was set to the "CL" (Climb) position instead of the "IDLE" position, which resulted in asymmetric thrust.

In a typical landing scenario, both thrust levers should be set to "IDLE" to allow the aircraft to decelerate using its brakes and spoilers. However, in this case, the right engine remained at high power, while the left engine's thrust was reduced. This created a significant thrust asymmetry, making it extremely difficult for the pilots to control the aircraft. The A320's design and safety protocols should have prevented such an error, but the investigation revealed that the right thrust lever's faulty setting was not adequately indicated to the pilots, leading to confusion and an inability to rectify the situation in time.

Additionally, the lack of runway grooves exacerbated the problem. Without the grooves, the runway's surface was more prone to hydroplaning, where a thin layer of water reduces friction and hinders braking efficiency. This meant that even under normal circumstances, the braking performance would have been compromised, but with the thrust asymmetry, it became a recipe for disaster.

The CENIPA report also highlighted issues with pilot training and communication. It pointed out that the pilots might not have been fully prepared to handle such an emergency, as they were not adequately trained to recognize and respond to the specific situation they encountered. Moreover, there were lapses in cockpit communication, with the pilots not effectively coordinating their actions during the critical moments of the landing.

Following the accident, several measures were implemented to prevent a recurrence of such a tragedy. TAM Airlines revised its pilot training programs to emphasize the correct use of thrust levers and better handling of abnormal situations. The airline also worked with Airbus to enhance the A320's systems to provide clearer indications of thrust lever positions to the flight crew.

Congonhas Airport faced scrutiny as well, with immediate efforts to improve runway safety. The runway was closed for grooving to enhance water drainage and braking performance, and stricter regulations were enforced regarding runway conditions during wet weather. These measures were aimed at ensuring that the airport could safely handle the high volume of traffic it experiences, particularly during adverse weather conditions.

The TAM Airlines Flight 3054 disaster remains a somber chapter in aviation history. It underscored the critical importance of precise aircraft operation, rigorous pilot training, and robust airport infrastructure. The lessons learned from this tragedy have contributed to enhancing aviation safety standards globally, with the hope of preventing similar accidents in the future. Despite the immense loss, the changes implemented in the wake of the crash have made air travel safer, honoring the memory of those who perished in this devastating event.

Chapter 45: ValuJet Flight 592

ValuJet Flight 592 was a scheduled domestic passenger flight from Miami International Airport in Miami, Florida, to Hartsfield-Jackson Atlanta International Airport in Atlanta, Georgia. On May 11, 1996, the McDonnell Douglas DC-9-32 operating the flight crashed into the Florida Everglades shortly after takeoff, resulting in the deaths of all 110 people on board. The tragedy exposed severe lapses in airline safety practices and regulatory oversight, leading to significant changes in the aviation industry.

The aircraft involved, a McDonnell Douglas DC-9-32, had a long service history before being operated by ValuJet. Originally built in 1969, it had changed hands multiple times and accumulated significant flight hours and cycles, indicative of its extensive use. ValuJet, a low-cost carrier founded in 1992, had rapidly expanded its fleet by acquiring older aircraft from various sources. The airline aimed to offer budget-friendly fares but faced numerous safety and maintenance issues, which would later be scrutinized in the wake of the crash.

On the morning of May 11, 1996, Flight 592 was scheduled to depart Miami at 13:00 EDT. The aircraft carried 105 passengers and 5 crew members, including Captain Candalyn Kubeck and First Officer Richard Hazen. Captain Kubeck was an experienced pilot with over 8,900 flight hours, and First Officer Hazen had logged approximately 4,200 hours. Both pilots were familiar with the DC-9 and had completed their mandatory training and certifications.

As the DC-9 taxied and prepared for takeoff, everything seemed routine. However, unbeknownst to the crew and passengers, a lethal danger lurked in the cargo hold. The plane was carrying a shipment of expired chemical oxygen generators, which had been improperly handled and packaged by SabreTech, a maintenance contractor. These oxygen generators, designed to provide emergency oxygen to passengers in the event of cabin depressurization, contained chemicals that could generate intense heat if activated. Critically, they were not equipped with safety caps to prevent accidental activation.

At approximately 14:04, ValuJet Flight 592 took off from runway 9L. Just six minutes into the flight, a fire broke out in the forward cargo hold. The oxygen generators, packed in boxes, had ignited, producing a fierce and uncontrollable blaze. Smoke quickly began to fill the cabin, and passengers and crew faced the terrifying realization that something was drastically wrong. Captain Kubeck and First Officer Hazen immediately initiated emergency procedures, declaring an emergency and requesting an immediate return to Miami.

The situation rapidly deteriorated. The fire in the cargo hold, fueled by the oxygen generators, produced thick smoke and intense heat, compromising the aircraft's structural integrity and systems. The cockpit voice recorder (CVR) captured the frantic efforts of the pilots as they tried to control the situation. Amidst the chaos, the pilots struggled to see through the smoke and maintain control of the aircraft, which had become increasingly unresponsive.

At 14:13, just eleven minutes after takeoff, Flight 592 crashed into the remote and swampy area of the Florida Everglades, about 10 miles northwest of Miami International Airport. The impact was catastrophic, and the aircraft disintegrated on impact, leaving a massive debris field and a smoldering fire that continued to burn in the aftermath. The remote location of the crash site, surrounded by water and dense vegetation, complicated rescue and recovery efforts.

All 110 people on board perished in the crash, and the impact of the disaster extended far beyond the immediate loss of life. The investigation, led by the National Transportation Safety Board (NTSB), sought to uncover the factors that led to the tragedy. The NTSB's findings revealed a series of alarming safety violations and regulatory oversights.

The oxygen generators, classified as hazardous materials, were not supposed to be transported on passenger aircraft unless properly deactivated and packed. SabreTech had failed to ensure the generators were safe for transport, and ValuJet, despite being responsible for the cargo on its aircraft, had not enforced stringent checks. The investigation exposed a lack of proper documentation, inadequate training for handling hazardous materials, and a broader culture of negligence within the airline and its contractors.

The NTSB's report highlighted multiple failures in the regulatory framework governing airline safety. The Federal Aviation Administration (FAA) had been criticized for its oversight of ValuJet, which had a history of maintenance issues and safety violations. Despite these red flags, the airline had continued to operate without significant intervention from regulators. The crash of Flight 592 underscored the need for more robust enforcement of safety regulations and better oversight of both airlines and maintenance contractors.

In the aftermath of the disaster, ValuJet faced severe scrutiny and public outrage. The airline's image was irreparably damaged, leading to a drastic decline in passenger confidence and financial instability. In an effort to salvage its operations, ValuJet merged with AirTran Airways in 1997, adopting the AirTran name and eventually becoming part of Southwest Airlines in 2014.

The crash of ValuJet Flight 592 also prompted substantial regulatory changes. The FAA implemented stricter regulations for the transportation of hazardous materials and increased oversight of airline maintenance practices. The incident served as a grim reminder of the consequences of cutting corners in aviation safety and the vital importance of rigorous adherence to safety protocols.

The legacy of Flight 592 is a stark testament to the need for vigilance in aviation safety. The lives lost in the Everglades crash were a heavy toll, but the lessons learned from the disaster led to significant improvements in the industry's approach to safety and regulation. The tragedy highlighted the interdependence of various components of the aviation system—airlines, maintenance contractors, and regulatory bodies—and the critical need for each to perform their roles with the utmost diligence to ensure the safety of passengers and crew.

The story of ValuJet Flight 592 remains a poignant chapter in aviation history, serving as a reminder of the human cost of negligence and the ongoing need for stringent safety measures in the airline industry. The improvements in safety protocols and regulatory oversight that followed have undoubtedly made air travel safer, preventing similar tragedies and honoring the memory of those who perished on that fateful day.

Chapter 46: Garuda Indonesia Flight 152

Garuda Indonesia Flight 152 was a scheduled domestic passenger flight from Jakarta to Medan, Indonesia. On September 26, 1997, the Airbus A300B4-220 operating the flight crashed into a wooded area near Medan, resulting in the deaths of all 234 passengers and crew on board. This tragic accident remains the deadliest aviation disaster in Indonesia's history and has had profound implications for aviation safety in the region.

The aircraft, an Airbus A300B4-220 registered PK-GAI, was relatively new, having been delivered to Garuda Indonesia in 1994. It had a strong safety record and was considered a reliable aircraft. The flight crew consisted of Captain Tsuwaya Manan, an experienced pilot with over 20,000 flight hours, and First Officer Pepsi Hadiyanto, who had accumulated more than 5,000 hours of flying experience. Both pilots were well-versed in the A300 and had extensive experience flying in and out of Medan's Polonia Airport.

Flight 152 departed from Jakarta's Soekarno-Hatta International Airport at 09:13 WIB, carrying 222 passengers and 12 crew members. The flight was uneventful until its approach to Medan. At the time, the region was experiencing severe haze caused by widespread forest fires in Sumatra and Kalimantan, significantly reducing visibility. The haze was so dense that it had already disrupted numerous flights and posed a serious challenge to the safe operation of aircraft in the area.

As Flight 152 approached Medan, it was cleared by air traffic control (ATC) to descend and prepare for landing. The crew received instructions to perform an instrument landing system (ILS) approach to runway 05. However, communication issues between the flight crew and ATC began to surface. The ATC, handling multiple flights simultaneously in poor visibility, provided directions that were misunderstood by the pilots, leading to confusion.

The critical moment came when ATC instructed the flight to turn left to heading 240 degrees to intercept the ILS localizer. However, the crew mistakenly turned right instead of left. This crucial error put the aircraft on a collision course with terrain. Despite repeated instructions from ATC to correct their heading, the miscommunication persisted, further complicating the situation.

The combination of low visibility due to the haze, communication misunderstandings, and the crew's confusion about their exact position created a perilous scenario. As the aircraft descended through 3,000 feet, the ground proximity warning system (GPWS) sounded, alerting the crew to the imminent danger of terrain collision. The pilots responded by attempting to pull up and increase altitude, but it was too late. At 13:30 local time, Flight 152 crashed into a forested area near the village of Buah Nabar, approximately 18 miles (30 kilometers) from Medan.

The impact was catastrophic. The aircraft was completely destroyed, and there were no survivors. The crash site, located in a densely forested area, made rescue operations challenging. Recovery teams faced significant difficulties navigating the rugged terrain and dense vegetation to retrieve bodies and wreckage. The scene was one of utter devastation, with debris scattered over a wide area and fires burning amidst the wreckage.

The investigation into the crash of Garuda Indonesia Flight 152 was led by the National Transportation Safety Committee (NTSC) of Indonesia, with assistance from international aviation experts, including the National Transportation Safety Board (NTSB) of the United States and representatives from Airbus. The investigation sought to determine the root causes of the accident and to provide recommendations to prevent similar tragedies in the future.

The NTSC's final report identified several critical factors that contributed to the crash. One of the primary causes was the miscommunication between the flight crew and ATC. The report highlighted that the controllers' instructions were ambiguous and, at times, unclear, leading to confusion in the cockpit. The dense haze severely limited visibility, exacerbating the crew's difficulty in maintaining situational awareness and accurately interpreting ATC directives.

The investigation also pointed to issues with the ATC system itself. At the time, Medan's Polonia Airport was not equipped with modern radar systems that could provide precise tracking of aircraft positions. This lack of advanced radar technology made it challenging for controllers to monitor and guide flights accurately, especially in poor visibility conditions. The NTSC recommended the urgent upgrade of ATC infrastructure, including the installation of advanced radar and communication systems, to enhance the safety and efficiency of flight operations.

Human factors also played a significant role in the accident. The report noted that the flight crew may have experienced cognitive overload due to the high-stress environment created by the low visibility and the complex instructions from ATC. This stress likely impaired their ability to process information accurately and respond appropriately to the unfolding situation. The NTSC emphasized the need for improved training programs for pilots and controllers, focusing on effective communication and decision-making in challenging conditions.

Another critical factor was the lack of standardized procedures for handling low-visibility operations. The investigation found that there were no clear guidelines for both flight crews and ATC on how to manage flights in severe haze conditions. This lack of standardization contributed to the confusion and miscommunication that ultimately led to the crash. The NTSC recommended the development and implementation of standardized low-visibility procedures to ensure that all parties involved in flight operations have a clear and consistent approach to managing such situations.

The crash of Garuda Indonesia Flight 152 had far-reaching implications for aviation safety in Indonesia and beyond. The recommendations from the NTSC's investigation led to significant changes in the country's aviation regulations and practices. The Indonesian government invested in upgrading ATC infrastructure, including the installation of advanced radar systems at major airports. These improvements enhanced the ability of controllers to monitor and guide aircraft accurately, even in adverse weather conditions.

In addition, the government mandated stricter adherence to safety protocols and enhanced training programs for both pilots and controllers. Airlines were required to implement comprehensive training programs that emphasized effective communication, decision-making, and situational awareness. These measures aimed to equip flight crews with the skills and knowledge needed to handle complex and challenging flight scenarios safely.

Internationally, the crash of Flight 152 underscored the importance of clear and unambiguous communication between flight crews and ATC. The International Civil Aviation Organization (ICAO) and other aviation regulatory bodies took note of the findings and recommendations from the investigation. They emphasized the need for standardized communication protocols and the implementation of advanced ATC technologies to enhance the safety of global aviation operations.

The legacy of Garuda Indonesia Flight 152 is a sobering reminder of the critical importance of communication, training, and infrastructure in ensuring the safety of air travel. The lessons learned from this tragic accident have contributed to significant improvements in aviation safety standards, helping to prevent similar disasters in the future. While the loss of 234 lives remains a profound tragedy, the changes implemented in the wake of the crash serve as a testament to the ongoing efforts to make air travel safer for everyone.

Chapter 47: AeroMexico Flight 498

Aeroméxico Flight 498, also known as the Cerritos mid-air collision, was a scheduled passenger flight from Mexico City to Los Angeles with several intermediate stops. On August 31, 1986, the McDonnell Douglas DC-9-32 operating the flight collided with a Piper PA-28-181 Archer, a private aircraft, over Cerritos, California. The disaster resulted in the deaths of all 67 people on the DC-9, the three people on the Piper, and 15 people on the ground, marking one of the most catastrophic aviation accidents in U.S. history.

The Aeroméxico DC-9, registration XA-JED, was on the last leg of its journey from Tijuana to Los Angeles International Airport (LAX). The flight had 58 passengers and 6 crew members on board, including Captain Arturo Valdes Prom, First Officer Jose Hector Valencia, and four flight attendants. The crew had substantial experience, with the captain amassing over 10,000 flight hours.

On that Sunday afternoon, the skies over Los Angeles were busy with commercial and private aviation traffic. The Piper PA-28, registered N4891F, was a single-engine aircraft piloted by William Kramer, with his wife and daughter as passengers. They were on a pleasure flight from Torrance to Big Bear City in Southern California.

At approximately 11:52 AM PDT, the Piper was flying at an altitude of 6,500 feet when it entered the Los Angeles Terminal Control Area (TCA) without proper clearance. Simultaneously, Aeroméxico Flight 498 was descending from 10,000 feet to 7,000 feet, under the control of LAX approach. The busy airspace, coupled with the lack of collision avoidance technology on both aircraft, set the stage for a disaster.

The two aircraft collided at an altitude of about 6,560 feet over Cerritos. The vertical stabilizer and left horizontal stabilizer of the DC-9 were sheared off by the Piper's propeller. The Piper was completely destroyed by the impact, killing all three occupants instantly. The severely damaged DC-9 entered an uncontrollable dive and crashed into a residential neighborhood in Cerritos.

The crash site in Cerritos was a scene of utter devastation. The DC-9 impacted in a densely populated area, destroying several homes and causing a massive fire. All 64 passengers and 6 crew members on the DC-9 perished in the crash, and 15 people on the ground were killed. The destruction of homes and the ensuing fire left a grim tableau of charred remains and wreckage. The local fire department and emergency responders faced significant challenges in extinguishing the blaze and recovering bodies from the debris.

The National Transportation Safety Board (NTSB) launched an exhaustive investigation into the mid-air collision. The final report identified several critical factors contributing to the disaster. One of the primary causes was the unauthorized entry of the Piper into the Los Angeles TCA without the required clearance. This violation of controlled airspace regulations placed the Piper on a collision course with the descending DC-9.

The NTSB also highlighted deficiencies in air traffic control (ATC) procedures and communication. The air traffic controllers managing the busy airspace around LAX were unable to detect the impending collision due to limitations in radar technology and the high workload. Additionally, the controllers were not alerted to the Piper's unauthorized presence in the TCA in time to take corrective action.

Another significant factor was the lack of collision avoidance technology on both aircraft. At the time, commercial aircraft were not yet equipped with the Traffic Collision Avoidance System (TCAS), which provides alerts to pilots about potential mid-air collisions and suggests evasive maneuvers. Similarly, general aviation aircraft like the Piper were not required to have transponders with altitude encoding, which would have provided more precise altitude information to ATC.

The NTSB's investigation also examined the regulatory environment governing airspace and aircraft equipment. The report recommended several changes to improve the safety of air travel, particularly in congested airspace. One of the key recommendations was the mandatory installation of TCAS on all commercial aircraft to provide real-time collision avoidance alerts. This technology, once implemented, would significantly reduce the risk of mid-air collisions by enhancing situational awareness for pilots and controllers.

Another recommendation was to require all general aviation aircraft operating in controlled airspace to be equipped with transponders that include altitude encoding. This change would allow ATC to more accurately monitor the positions and altitudes of all aircraft, thereby improving traffic separation and reducing the risk of collisions.

The Cerritos mid-air collision also led to a re-evaluation of air traffic control procedures and training. The NTSB recommended enhancements to controller training programs, emphasizing the importance of situational awareness and effective communication. Additionally, the FAA was urged to review and update its regulations governing airspace management to ensure that controllers have the necessary tools and support to manage busy airspace safely.

In the aftermath of the disaster, the aviation community implemented several key changes to improve safety. The FAA mandated the installation of TCAS on all commercial aircraft, a move that was fully implemented in the following years. This system has since proven to be a vital tool in preventing mid-air collisions and enhancing overall air traffic safety.

For general aviation, the requirement for altitude-encoding transponders became more stringent, improving the accuracy of aircraft tracking by ATC. This change has helped reduce the risk of unauthorized airspace incursions and improved the overall safety of air traffic operations.

The tragic events of Aeroméxico Flight 498 also had a profound impact on the residents of Cerritos and the broader aviation community. The loss of life and destruction caused by the crash prompted efforts to improve emergency response and disaster preparedness in residential areas near airports. Communities and local authorities worked together to develop better emergency plans and improve coordination with aviation authorities to enhance safety for residents living near busy flight paths.

The legacy of the Cerritos mid-air collision continues to influence aviation safety practices today. The lessons learned from this disaster have contributed to significant advancements in collision avoidance technology, air traffic control procedures, and regulatory frameworks. The implementation of TCAS and the improved tracking of general aviation aircraft have made the skies safer for both passengers and pilots.

While the memory of the 82 lives lost in the Cerritos tragedy remains a somber reminder of the potential dangers of air travel, the changes implemented in the wake of the disaster serve as a testament to the ongoing efforts to improve aviation safety. The Cerritos mid-air collision underscores the critical importance of effective communication, robust technology, and stringent regulations in ensuring the safety of the global aviation system.

Chapter 48: Nigerian Airways Flight 2120

Nigerian Airways Flight 2120 was a tragic aviation disaster that occurred on July 11, 1991, involving a chartered flight operated by Nationair Canada on behalf of Nigerian Airways. The flight was scheduled to transport Hajj pilgrims from Jeddah, Saudi Arabia, to Sokoto, Nigeria. The aircraft, a Douglas DC-8-61, encountered catastrophic issues shortly after takeoff from Jeddah's King Abdulaziz International Airport, leading to a fire on board and the eventual crash of the plane. All 261 passengers and crew perished in the incident, marking it as one of the deadliest aviation disasters involving a Canadian airline and in Saudi Arabian airspace.

The aircraft involved in the disaster was a Douglas DC-8-61, registered as C-GMXQ. This aircraft, manufactured in 1968, had a long service history and had been leased by Nationair Canada to Nigerian Airways for the Hajj pilgrimage season. The crew on board included Captain William Allan, First Officer Kent Davidge, and Flight Engineer Victor Fehr, along with 13 flight attendants. The crew was experienced and had undergone the necessary training to handle the DC-8 aircraft.

On the morning of July 11, 1991, Flight 2120 was scheduled to depart Jeddah for Sokoto, carrying a full load of 247 passengers, mostly Nigerian pilgrims returning home after performing the Hajj pilgrimage. The aircraft taxied to the runway and took off at approximately 08:28 local time. However, immediately after takeoff, the crew experienced significant issues that would quickly escalate into a full-blown emergency.

Just minutes into the flight, the crew noticed a loss of cabin pressure, and the aircraft failed to climb as expected. Unbeknownst to the crew, the DC-8 had suffered a tire burst during takeoff. The tire debris had damaged a hydraulic line, causing hydraulic fluid to ignite and initiate a fire in the wheel well. This fire, initially contained within the wheel well, began to spread rapidly due to the continuous flow of oxygen.

As the aircraft struggled to climb, the flight engineer reported the loss of hydraulic pressure and difficulties controlling the aircraft's systems. The situation deteriorated quickly as the fire breached the fuselage, allowing smoke and flames to enter the cabin. Passengers and crew began to experience the effects of smoke inhalation, and the situation inside the aircraft became increasingly dire.

Despite the worsening conditions, Captain Allan and his crew attempted to return to King Abdulaziz International Airport for an emergency landing. The crew declared an emergency and communicated their intentions to air traffic control. However, the fire's intensity and the damage to the aircraft's systems made controlling the DC-8 exceedingly difficult. The cabin was rapidly filling with smoke, and the structural integrity of the aircraft was compromised by the spreading fire.

At approximately 08:35, just seven minutes after takeoff, the situation reached a critical point. The aircraft was now engulfed in flames, and the structural damage caused by the fire led to a catastrophic failure of the fuselage. The DC-8 entered an uncontrollable descent and crashed into the ground near the village of Suman, about 6 kilometers north of the airport. The impact and ensuing explosion resulted in the complete destruction of the aircraft.

The crash of Flight 2120 resulted in the deaths of all 261 people on board. The post-crash fire consumed much of the wreckage, making the recovery of bodies and the investigation into the cause of the disaster extremely challenging. Saudi Arabian authorities, along with international aviation experts, launched an immediate investigation to determine the cause of the accident and to identify any factors that could have contributed to the tragedy.

The investigation revealed several critical factors that led to the disaster. The initial cause of the fire was traced to the tire burst during takeoff. The tire failure was attributed to under-inflation, which caused excessive heat buildup and ultimately led to the tire bursting. The resulting debris damaged the hydraulic line, igniting the hydraulic fluid and initiating the fire.

Further investigation uncovered lapses in maintenance procedures and oversight. Nationair Canada, the operator of the aircraft, was found to have neglected proper maintenance protocols for the DC-8. The aircraft's maintenance records showed that the tire had been under-inflated for several days prior to the accident, and this condition had not been addressed. Additionally, there were issues with the aircraft's fire detection and suppression systems, which failed to contain the fire in its early stages.

The investigation also highlighted deficiencies in the crew's emergency response. While the crew attempted to manage the situation and return to the airport, the rapid spread of the fire and the resulting structural damage made it nearly impossible to control the aircraft. The lack of effective communication and coordination among the crew further exacerbated the emergency.

The disaster of Nigerian Airways Flight 2120 had far-reaching implications for the aviation industry. The findings of the investigation led to increased scrutiny of maintenance practices and regulatory oversight for charter operators and airlines. The International Civil Aviation Organization (ICAO) and other aviation regulatory bodies implemented stricter guidelines for aircraft maintenance, particularly concerning tire pressure management and the inspection of critical systems.

In Canada, the crash had a significant impact on Nationair Canada, which faced severe criticism and legal repercussions in the aftermath of the disaster. The airline's reputation was severely damaged, and it struggled to recover from the financial and legal fallout. Ultimately,

Nationair Canada ceased operations in 1993, unable to overcome the ramifications of the Flight 2120 disaster.

The legacy of Flight 2120 also led to advancements in aircraft safety technology. Improvements in fire detection and suppression systems were mandated, ensuring that fires originating in areas such as wheel wells could be detected and contained more effectively. Enhanced materials and design changes were implemented to reduce the risk of fires spreading to critical areas of the aircraft.

The tragedy also underscored the importance of crew training and emergency preparedness. Airlines worldwide revisited their training programs to ensure that flight crews were better equipped to handle in-flight emergencies, including fires and loss of cabin pressure. The emphasis on effective communication and coordination among crew members during emergencies became a focal point of training programs.

For the families of the victims, the disaster of Nigerian Airways Flight 2120 was a devastating loss. The memory of the 261 lives lost in the crash serves as a poignant reminder of the importance of rigorous maintenance practices, regulatory oversight, and continuous improvements in aviation safety. The lessons learned from this tragic event have contributed to enhancing the safety of air travel, ensuring that such a disaster is less likely to occur in the future.

Chapter 49: Asiana Airlines Flight 214

Asiana Airlines Flight 214 was a scheduled transpacific passenger flight from Incheon International Airport near Seoul, South Korea, to San Francisco International Airport in California, United States. On July 6, 2013, the Boeing 777-200ER operating this flight crashed during its final approach to San Francisco. The crash resulted in the deaths of three passengers and injured 187 others, making it one of the most serious aviation accidents in the United States in recent years. This incident drew significant attention and led to a comprehensive investigation by the National Transportation Safety Board (NTSB) to understand the causes and contributing factors.

The aircraft involved was a Boeing 777-200ER, registration HL7742, which had been in service since March 2006. The plane was equipped with modern avionics and safety systems, and Asiana Airlines, the operator, was known for its strong safety record. On board Flight 214 were 291 passengers and 16 crew members, including Captain Lee Kang-kook, who was in command during the landing, Captain Lee Jeong-min, who was acting as a training captain, and First Officer Bong Dong-won, along with a relief first officer.

Flight 214 departed Incheon International Airport on July 5, 2013, at 16:35 KST, bound for San Francisco. The flight proceeded uneventfully for most of its journey across the Pacific Ocean. As the aircraft neared the West Coast of the United States, it began its descent into San Francisco International Airport under visual flight rules (VFR) conditions, with clear skies and good visibility.

The trouble began during the final approach to runway 28L at San Francisco. The glide slope portion of the instrument landing system (ILS) was out of service due to airport maintenance, and the crew was conducting a visual approach using the Precision Approach Path Indicator (PAPI) lights to guide their descent. Despite the good weather and visibility, the approach became unstable.

The aircraft was significantly below the optimal glide path as it approached the runway. The pilots failed to maintain the necessary airspeed and altitude, resulting in the aircraft descending too rapidly and being too low. The automated systems on the Boeing 777, including the autothrottle, were not properly managed, contributing to the low speed.

At an altitude of approximately 500 feet, the airspeed dropped to 112 knots, significantly below the target approach speed of 137 knots. The pilots recognized the issue and attempted to correct it by increasing thrust, but their actions were too late. The aircraft continued to descend below the glide path, and at 11:27 AM PDT, the main landing gear and tail struck the seawall at the threshold of runway 28L. This initial impact caused the tail section to separate from the fuselage, and the aircraft skidded along the runway before coming to a stop.

The impact and subsequent skidding caused severe structural damage to the aircraft. The tail section and landing gear were destroyed, and a fire broke out in the fuselage. Despite the catastrophic damage, the fuselage remained largely intact, allowing many passengers to survive the initial impact. However, three passengers were killed: two died from injuries sustained during the crash, and one was run over by a rescue vehicle responding to the scene.

The evacuation of the aircraft was chaotic but largely successful, with many passengers escaping through emergency slides and exits. The fire, fueled by spilled jet fuel, engulfed the rear section of the plane, but firefighters were able to bring it under control before it spread to the entire fuselage. Emergency responders faced significant challenges due to the damaged state of the aircraft and the need to quickly assist injured passengers.

The NTSB conducted a thorough investigation to determine the causes of the crash. The investigation revealed several critical factors that contributed to the accident. One of the primary findings was that the flight crew mismanaged the approach and failed to maintain the proper airspeed and altitude. The pilots' reliance on automated systems, without fully understanding their operation, was a significant factor. The autothrottle system, which should have helped maintain the correct airspeed, was not properly engaged, leading to the aircraft's low speed and subsequent stall.

The investigation also highlighted deficiencies in pilot training and communication. Captain Lee Kang-kook was undergoing training for his initial operating experience on the Boeing 777 and was being supervised by Captain Lee Jeong-min. The cockpit resource management (CRM) during the approach was inadequate, with insufficient communication and coordination between the pilots. The training captain did not effectively monitor and assist the trainee pilot, and the first officer did not adequately alert the captain to the deteriorating situation.

Another critical factor was the absence of the ILS glide slope, which required the pilots to rely on visual cues and manual control to maintain the correct approach path. The lack of ILS glide slope increased the workload on the pilots and contributed to the unstable approach. The NTSB emphasized the need for pilots to be proficient in manual flying skills and to effectively manage automated systems, especially in conditions where automated aids are unavailable.

The NTSB also examined the role of the aircraft's automated systems and the design of the autothrottle. The investigation found that the autothrottle system had a mode known as "HOLD" mode, which disengaged active speed control when the aircraft was below 400 feet during landing. This mode, coupled with the lack of proper monitoring by the pilots, allowed the airspeed to drop dangerously low. The NTSB recommended that Boeing review and improve the design of the autothrottle system to prevent similar incidents.

In its final report, the NTSB made several recommendations to improve aviation safety. These included enhancing pilot training programs to emphasize manual flying skills and the effective management of automated systems, improving cockpit resource management to ensure better communication and coordination among flight crew members, and reviewing and redesigning automated systems to prevent disengagement of critical functions during landing.

The Asiana Airlines Flight 214 crash had significant implications for the aviation industry. The lessons learned from this accident led to changes in training programs and procedures for airlines worldwide. Emphasis was placed on ensuring that pilots are proficient in manual flying skills and understand the operation of automated systems. The importance of effective communication and coordination among flight crew members was reinforced, with a focus on improving CRM training.

In response to the NTSB's recommendations, Boeing reviewed and made changes to the design of the autothrottle system to address the issues identified in the investigation. These changes aimed to prevent the disengagement of active speed control during critical phases of flight, such as landing. Additionally, the Federal Aviation Administration (FAA) and other regulatory bodies reviewed and updated their guidelines and regulations to enhance pilot training and improve the monitoring of automated systems.

The crash of Flight 214 also led to a renewed focus on airport safety and emergency response procedures. San Francisco International Airport and other airports around the world reviewed and updated their emergency response plans to ensure that rescue and firefighting teams are better prepared to handle similar incidents. The importance of swift and coordinated emergency response was emphasized to minimize the impact of future accidents.

For the families of the victims and the survivors of Flight 214, the crash was a traumatic and life-changing event. The loss of life and the injuries sustained in the crash left a lasting impact on all those affected. Asiana Airlines provided compensation to the victims and their families and worked to support them in the aftermath of the disaster.

In the broader context of aviation safety, the crash of Asiana Airlines Flight 214 serves as a reminder of the complexities and challenges of modern air travel. The incident highlighted the need for continuous improvement in pilot training, the effective management of automated systems, and the importance of communication and coordination in the cockpit. The lessons learned from this tragedy have contributed to making air travel safer for passengers and crew members worldwide.

Chapter 50: Cubana de Aviación Flight 455

Cubana de Aviación Flight 455 was a scheduled passenger flight from Barbados to Jamaica, which met a tragic end on October 6, 1976. The flight, operated by a Douglas DC-8, was en route from Barbados' Seawell Airport (now Grantley Adams International Airport) to Kingston, Jamaica, with previous stops in Guyana and Trinidad. This flight became the center of an international incident when it was brought down by a terrorist bomb, resulting in the deaths of all 73 people on board. The event remains one of the most significant and deadly acts of terrorism in aviation history, highlighting the geopolitical tensions of the Cold War era and the struggle between the United States and Cuba.

Cubana Flight 455 began its journey in Guyana, making stops in Trinidad and Tobago before reaching Barbados, where it was scheduled to fly onward to Kingston, Jamaica, and then Havana, Cuba. The aircraft was a Douglas DC-8, a four-engine jet airliner, with a crew of five and 68 passengers on board. Among the passengers were several Cuban citizens, including young athletes from the Cuban national fencing team, Guyanese medical students on scholarships to study in Cuba, and North Korean nationals.

On the morning of October 6, 1976, the flight departed Seawell Airport at 11:21 AM, bound for Kingston. The takeoff was uneventful, and the aircraft climbed to its cruising altitude. However, just nine minutes into the flight, two bombs hidden in the aircraft's rear lavatories exploded. The bombs had been placed on the plane during a stopover in Trinidad by two Venezuelans, Hernán Ricardo Lozano and Freddy Lugo, who had connections to anti-Castro Cuban exiles.

The explosions caused an immediate loss of control as the rear of the aircraft was severely damaged, leading to a fire in the cabin. The flight crew, led by Captain Wilfredo Pérez Pérez, First Officer Miguel Espinosa, Flight Engineer Ernesto Machín, and Navigators Jesús Mulet and Lázaro Medina, attempted to return to Seawell Airport. Despite their efforts, the structural integrity of the DC-8 was compromised, and the fire spread rapidly. The pilots reported the emergency to air traffic control, and their distress calls were recorded. Captain Pérez's final words, "We are descending immediately! We have a fire on board!" and "Patria o muerte, venceremos!" (Homeland or death, we shall overcome!) were a testament to their desperate struggle to save the aircraft and its passengers.

The DC-8 lost altitude quickly and crashed into the sea about eight kilometers west of the coast of Barbados. All 73 passengers and crew members perished in the crash. The tragic loss included 24 members of the Cuban national fencing team, returning from a successful competition in Venezuela, where they had won gold medals. The crash was devastating for Cuba, leading to national mourning and an outpouring of grief and anger.

In the immediate aftermath of the bombing, the governments of Cuba and Barbados launched investigations. Divers and recovery teams retrieved wreckage and bodies from the crash site, and forensic examinations confirmed the presence of explosive residues, indicating that bombs had caused the disaster. The international community was quick to condemn the attack, and attention soon focused on the two Venezuelans, Hernán Ricardo Lozano and Freddy Lugo, who were apprehended in Trinidad just before they could escape to the United States.

The investigation revealed that the bombs had been smuggled onto the aircraft with the help of anti-Castro Cuban exiles operating out of Venezuela and the United States. The mastermind behind the bombing was identified as Luis Posada Carriles, a former CIA operative with a long history of anti-Castro activities. Alongside him was Orlando Bosch, another prominent anti-Castro militant. Both men had been involved in various plots against the Cuban government and were known for their violent tactics.

Posada Carriles and Bosch had connections with the Coordination of United Revolutionary Organizations (CORU), an umbrella group of anti-Castro organizations that had conducted numerous terrorist attacks against Cuban targets. The bombing of Cubana Flight 455 was part of a broader campaign to destabilize the Cuban government and to deter countries in the Caribbean and Latin America from maintaining relations with Havana.

The arrest and prosecution of the individuals involved in the bombing were complex and politically charged. Lozano and Lugo were tried and convicted in Venezuela, receiving long prison sentences. However, the extradition and prosecution of Posada Carriles and Bosch proved more difficult. Posada Carriles managed to escape from a Venezuelan prison in 1985 while awaiting a retrial and fled to Central America. He continued his anti-Castro activities, including involvement in bombings in Havana in the late 1990s.

Orlando Bosch, after being held and acquitted in Venezuela, returned to the United States, where he faced various legal battles but eventually received a presidential pardon from George H.W. Bush in 1990, allowing him to live freely in Miami. This pardon was heavily criticized by Cuba and several human rights organizations, who viewed Bosch as a terrorist.

The bombing of Cubana Flight 455 had profound repercussions. It highlighted the intensity of the Cold War-era conflict between the United States and Cuba, and the extent to which anti-Castro militants were willing to go to achieve their goals. The attack also strained relations between the United States and several Caribbean and Latin American countries, who condemned the use of terrorism and criticized the perceived leniency of the U.S. towards anti-Castro exiles.

In Cuba, the incident reinforced the government's narrative of being under constant threat from the United States and its allies. The

Cuban government used the bombing to rally national support and to justify its policies of tight internal security and vigilance against external threats. The memory of the victims, particularly the young athletes, became a symbol of Cuban resistance and martyrdom.

The attack also led to changes in aviation security. The international community recognized the need for stronger measures to prevent similar acts of terrorism. This included improved screening and security protocols at airports, better coordination between intelligence agencies to monitor and intercept potential threats, and stricter regulations regarding the transportation of hazardous materials.

Despite these measures, the quest for justice for the victims of Cubana Flight 455 remained fraught with challenges. Luis Posada Carriles, the mastermind behind the bombing, continued to evade prosecution for many years. He was detained in the United States in 2005 on charges of illegal entry but was not extradited to Venezuela or Cuba to face charges related to the bombing. Posada Carriles lived in Miami until his death in 2018, never facing full accountability for his role in the attack.

The legacy of Cubana Flight 455 continues to resonate today. It serves as a stark reminder of the destructive power of terrorism and the enduring impact of political violence. The families of the victims have kept their memories alive through memorials and advocacy for justice. In Cuba, the incident is commemorated annually, with ceremonies honoring the lives lost and condemning the acts of terrorism that led to their deaths.

Epilogue

As we close the pages of "True Stories of Aviation Disasters & Mysteries," we reflect on the myriad emotions these accounts have stirred. From the haunting mysteries of vanished flights to the harrowing details of catastrophic failures, each story has offered a glimpse into the fragile balance between human ambition and the uncontrollable forces of nature and fate.

The journey through these fifty chapters has not only been a recounting of events but a profound exploration of the human spirit's resilience. We have seen the tireless dedication of investigators who comb through wreckage for clues, the bravery of passengers and crew in the face of disaster, and the grief and strength of families seeking closure. These stories remind us that every disaster impacts real lives, leaving an indelible mark on communities and shaping the course of aviation history.

Advancements in aviation technology and safety protocols have often been born from tragedy. Each incident has propelled us to ask difficult questions and seek innovative solutions. Black box recorders, improved aircraft design, rigorous safety checks, and comprehensive pilot training are just a few of the measures that have emerged from the lessons learned. While these advancements cannot erase the past, they serve as a testament to our commitment to making the skies safer.

Yet, despite our best efforts, mysteries still linger. The fate of Amelia Earhart remains an enigma, and the disappearance of Malaysia Airlines Flight MH370 continues to baffle experts. These unresolved cases challenge our understanding and push us to keep searching for answers, driven by the hope that one day, technology and perseverance will illuminate the unknown.

As we move forward, the stories contained within this book should serve as both a caution and an inspiration. They remind us of the importance of vigilance, innovation, and compassion. They urge us to honor those lost by continuing to strive for excellence and safety in aviation. Each flight we take today is a testament to the sacrifices and lessons of the past.

In closing, let us carry forward the memory of these events not as tales of despair but as narratives of human determination. Let us continue to seek the balance between the wonder of flight and the solemn respect for its risks. And above all, let us remain committed to the pursuit of knowledge, ensuring that the legacy of those who have been lost in the sky is one of continuous improvement and unwavering hope.

"True Stories of Aviation Disasters & Mysteries" stands as a reminder that the quest for understanding and the drive to overcome challenges are at the heart of human progress. As we look to the future of aviation, may we do so with a renewed commitment to safety, innovation, and the unyielding spirit of exploration that has always defined our journey through the skies.

The End.